MY DESTINY AGAINST THEIR LIES WHERE IS MY MOTHER?

MY DESTINY AGAINST THEIR LIES WHERE IS MY MOTHER?

Hamiye Oksuz

CONTENTS

1   1

2   2

1

MY DESTINY AGAINST THEIR LIES
WHERE IS MY MOTHER?
Hamiye Öksüz

This book is based on true stories. In order to respect their privacy, names of the characters were changed.

2

Hello, I'm Hamiye Öksüz. The reason behind this book is to share my regular thoughts and questions that I asked myself. And the misbeliefs of the society that inflict deep wounds... I would like express my feelings on these subjects. I do believe that, lie cannot benefit anyone at any cost. It's a word that lets people fall into abyss, and makes minds intoxicated...

Sometimes us, the people, cannot get what we want. We cannot always know what are the things that life had spared for us. Fighting a battle between what you want and the reality, fighting hard, but being the loser in the end, and finding yourself in a life that you have no desire... And sometimes there are some steps to take, some difficult steps, difficult to turn back, and some other steps that you are not ready to take in a young age! Steps that hinder your own childhood and youthfulness... In this life, there are some sets of events for each of us; being poor, losing your mother or your father, or falling ill... Each one of us might be a part of a fight in this life, because death is just the end of the time that was granted us by the hand of God. And diseases, are just some tests, that has been given to us from God. He tests our patience to remind us what is the true meaning of being healthy.

He helps people to shake things off and start over. Here are the notable events of your destiny: Coming into the world; you cannot choose your own family. You cannot stop death! Birth, and death are the destiny itself. But the things happening between birth and death, are they destiny or cost?

I'm one of those people who believe life is a test. And the only one subject that makes me feel sad, is the actions of society, that focus on their own benefits but not the human life. And dragging the religion into this fight is just another aspect of this problem… So, they connect many subjects into the destiny.

I was born in one of the villages in Bafta District of Samsun. For sure, I don't have the ability to remember what it was like when I was born. Anyway, my first memory as a child comes from the ages of 4-5. I started a war in the house. All of my brothers were going to school. I was at home. I was screaming to the ones at home "Why won't you let me go to the school?". They were telling me I was not at the age of a school girl, so that I should have waited. But I wasn't listening any of those. I needed to go to the school, just like everyone else…

We were five siblings. Except me, all of them were going to the school. I was dying to be just like them, to go to the school. I was taking their bags or school uniforms, and creating a problem. In the end my grandfather told me "Okay, you've won, let's go to the school". We were ready to go. We had to walk for thirty minutes to get to the school.

When we get there, my grandfather get permission from school principal for me to attend one of the classes of my brother as a guest student. Later I found out that, they made a decision to let me go to school for couple of days, so that I would get bored in the end, and didn't want to go again. My brother was at fifth grade. The subject was social studies. There was a written subject on the board, so I was trying to write the same thing to the paper. Luckily, I was able to write it almost correct just because I wanted to be there so bad. And then, other students right next to me called the teacher by saying; "Teacher, she's writing the same thing whatever we're writing but with her left hand". Teacher Sevda said "I was already expecting that, there must be an ability of you, because you wanted to be here so much". So, she turned them and said "Leave her be, don't distract yourself". When I asked her and other students about some letters that I didn't know, they all helped me so much with a great patience. That day, I was happy from head to toe. It was a day to remember, just because the excitement of that day...

It was time to go to home, so we left the school as a group of students. We all were walking together to our homes. Before we were half way through, I was already tired. My brother Ferhat looked at me and said "Come!". I got on his back, and then he carried me all the way back to home. I was sleeping when we get there. I slept so tight that, by the time I was awake it was already morning and my brothers were already gone. My grandmother said to me "You should rest today, tomorrow you can go again". I really needed a rest, but finally I was free. I would be able to go to the school again.

The day I stayed at home spent with me telling things about school. In the meantime, my grandfather was getting ready. He told my grandmother "I'm going to head out, do you need anything?". My grandfather was going to the mosque of the village for the Friday prayer. He, then asked me "Do you need anything?", and I told him, "I want gum!". My grandmother then said "My God accept your prayers, don't forget to buy what's been told to you!"

I didn't go to the school on Friday. On Saturdays, school were part-time. They told me, today's only part-time, you don't need to go. But I was determined so I went to the school. As the days passed, all of the teachers had the chance to test my abilities. And one day, they called my grandfather to talk about me at the office of the principal. After the talking, Nazlı Teacher called me and said "From now on, you're my student. But don't be late ever! I want to see you in the class every morning", and then kissed me. I was so happy. I was so excited that I hugged my grandfather's legs. Teachers told my grandfather "She's a great student, she learned how to read and write in a brief time, so we can't let her go". So that's how they decided to take me at school. I was at the same class of my older brother...

My teacher was pretty patient about me, and also, she was a great teacher. She always thought about her students. That year, some new teacher came to the school. In this way, we were able to have a teacher per class. So that meant whole system would be tidy.

In the meantime, we were getting ready for the school; school uniform, bag, notebooks, books... My aunt-in-law was the tailer of home. So, she was going to sew my uniform. She made all of us brand new uniforms.

We were going to the school as a pretty big group. There were many different people in the villages: People from Trabzon, Laz people, people from Salonica, other immigrants, Albanians... Albanian families and us, Laz families were in the same neighbourhood, so we were going to the school all the time. Our school was next to the neighbourhood of immigrants and people from Salonica. All of us were speaking Turkish pretty differently, our accents were different, but we were friends. Our school was the main thing that made us come closer.

Those were the years 1973-1974... Only my three brothers and I were going to the school. My older sister had already graduated from elementary school.

We were coming together and walking towards the school. We were almost 10-15 kids. Sometimes, due to the illness and other incidents, that number may have been gone down. We were having great conversations on the road. Sometimes we raced with each other on the way to the school. When we got there, teacher was always asking us why some of us not made it to

the school that day. And we told them the reason... We were running down to the creek, and from then on, we started walking because there was a hill.

After the school, we would always go to our grandfather with my older brother Mehmet. We would study, right next to our grandfather. My grandfather's radio was always open. He would usually listen Turkish classical music. When it was time for news, he would tell us "Be quiet, I'm going to listen the news". He didn't miss it, even a single time. After our study, our grandmother would always bring us boiled egg, or boiled corn. We loved to have both of them.

I also had a goal. Before I started school, my father came to visit us way back from Germany. When it was time to go back, he told my mother "Make my daughter ready, I want to take her with me", but my mother told him "Not without me", then my father said "Then you should come too", but my mother insisted "I would never go there", my father persisted "She would be a voice in the house, please come with me", but my mother was having none of it. He couldn't convince her. I was really affected, because my father was gone. I actually wanted to go with him, but when I realised it was getting problematic, I told him "Father, don't fight over this. We will come with my mother, when she decides to do". My father was really gone. My mother still insisted that she wouldn't go, and wouldn't let his girl to go either. I couldn't figure it out why my mother decided to stay, even though my father persisted it so much. I couldn't express any of my feeling, so that turned into the sense of ambition. I was eager to learn how to write, because I wanted to write to my father. There was a hole inside me, and I was trying to cover it with this ambition.

The hole inside me was actually the absence of my father. And while trying to cover this hole of my life, I learned how to write relatively quickly, and started to write my own letters to my father. My grandfather would go to the centre of the city every Monday, and I would write letter to my father those days. Firstly, I wrote about my school life. But then I started to talk about news from our village. One day my aunts saw me writing to my father. They asked me "What are you writing?", I answered "Letter to my father". Then with excitement they said "You are amazing, you are doing a good job for you and your father, tell our best regards to your father, tell him we are kissing his black eyes, ask him when will he come back?". Their eyes filled with tears. Being that far, in a foreign country, those are the reason of loneliness in their minds.

My father almost replied most of my letters, if not each one. But he replied my first ever letter to him pretty quickly. He probably surprised. He also sent ten liras of pocket money with his letter. He also wrote, "A friend of mine will come to see you in a short time to help you about your school raincoats". He then said "I'm thanking to my God, because he let me see you write to me with your tiny fingers" ... He also said, through his friend I should have recorded my reading in a tape. Each one of us at home, read that letter. It really affected us. We sent a reply quickly. We told him we were going to do the thing he wanted from us. My mother also wanted me to write something to my father through her words, so I wrote the things she told me.

After another day at school, we were getting ready to go to our houses. But we surprised, because it was snowy outside. We were happy about it. Of course, we started a snow ball fight immediately. Then we started to walk towards our village. When we came to the hill, my brother put his bag to the ground and said to me "Come behind me, hold tight to me!", and so I did. My brother slowly started to slide a bit. Then I thought we were flying! We slid, until we came closer to the creek. First, I didn't realise what was happening, but then I enjoyed it too much! My brother said "If we manage to come tomorrow, we'll slide again", and I said "Okay!". Of course, many of our friends slid with us.

I would usually become tired on the return way, and feel sleepy. I was just a kid, and I wouldn't sleep in afternoons, because we were at school. So, my brothers always did their best to return home before I felt sleepy. Sometimes, I wouldn't resist, and slept. Then I wouldn't even understand whether we came home or not. Of course, my brothers were not fond of these sleepy events of mine. They would always encourage me, by saying; "Come on, let's be patient, after this hill, it's home, try to resist!". I would always try my best, but couldn't find a way to resist the urge to sleep, and started to sway around. And finally, one of them would fall pity, and took me on their back.

That day, I was really happy. That exact day, my brother was like a real brother to me. He played with me, we slit on the snow. I asked him "So, are we going to be able to go to the school?", he told me "If it continues like this, it's not possible. So, the teachers wouldn't be able to go to the school, then they probably cancel today", and I asked him again "But how are we going to understand it is cancelled?", he said "Well, we understand if the roads are closed, and we probably can't hear it but, they announced it from the mosque".

It snowed till midnight. And as my brother said, all roads were closed due to the snow. But it was not a problem for neighbours. They couldn't go to shopping, but they provided their need of sugar, tea, salt, and flour from the spares in their warehouses. Because in the end, we were living in a village. We were not that far to the city, but sometimes roads would be closed down due to some natural event, so we would share our spares with our neighbours. When the weather cleared, everyone would pay their part. So, our relation as neighbours continued strongly. Three houses we're pretty close to each other (My grandfather's, my father's, and Uncle Bahri's). My uncle was the groom of Uncle Bahri. We would always ask each other, whether we have any problem, or any need. And its only reason was to be a good neighbour, and help others. So, thanks to the strong bonds, people were closer to each other back then. None of us were that rich, but sharing what you have was the indication of the value.

Every winter night, we would meet in a house, and had long and deep conversations. Conversations were mostly about old memories, history, politics, and economy. Main trade good of our village was tobacco. My grandfather's father learned the tobacco farming from a Jew from Batumi, Georgia. When my grandfather started to share his own memories about his young times, we would listen him, like watching an action movie.

home before I felt sleepy. Sometimes, I could not resist and slept. Then I would not even understand whether we came home or not. Of course, my brothers were not fond of these sleepy events of mine. They would always encourage me, by saying; "Come on, let's be patient, after this hill, it's home, try to resist!". I would always try my best, but could not find a way to resist the urge to sleep, and started to sway around. And finally, one of them would feel pity and take me on their back.

That day, I was happy. That exact day, my brother was like a real brother to me. He played with me, we slit on the snow. I asked him "So, are we going to be able to go to the school?", he told me "If it continues like this, it's not possible. So, the teachers would not be able to go to the school, then they probably cancel today", and I asked him again "But how are we going to understand it is cancelled?", he said, "Well, we understand if the roads are closed, and we probably can't hear it but, they announced it from the mosque".

It snowed till midnight. And as my brother said, all roads were closed due to the snow. But it was not a problem for neighbours. They could not go shopping, but they provided their need for sugar, tea, salt, and flour from the spares in their warehouses. Because in the end, we were living in a village. We were not that far from the city, but sometimes roads would be closed due to some natural event, so we would share our spares with our neighbours. When the weather cleared, everyone would pay their part. So, our relationship as neighbours continued strongly. Three houses we're pretty close to each other (My grandfather's, my father's, and Uncle Bahri's). My uncle was the groom of Uncle Bahri. We would always ask each other, whether we have any problems or any need. And its only reason was to be a good neighbour, and help others. So, thanks to the strong bonds, people were closer to each other back then. None of us were that rich, but sharing what you have was an indication of the value. quickly. So, I would always ask for bread and butter. And my grandmother would tell me "You should eat less" while preparing my buttered bread. Once, I asked my grandfather "Why I'm always getting hungry?", he smiled and said "You need to grow up, so that why you want to eat more. You have a small tummy, so that's why you eat less but frequently. And don't mind you grandmother, she's just messing with you, nothing that she doesn't want you to eat or something", and then they both smiled.

In that night, we had so much fun recording those tapes, but my aunt also got tired too much. After everyone went their places, we slept with my aunt on a mattress. In the late hours, I felt like I needed to go to the toilet. So, I called my aunt. But she was sleeping pretty deep. She just said, "Hmm hmm", and then with a loud voice I called her "Auntttt!". She woke up, and took me to the toilets, while holding the flashlight for me. I wear the clogs for the toilet, they were making sounds like tak tuk, tak tuk... After that I went straight to my bed. In the morning, I woke up to the sound of my aunt. She was saying "I washed you before, but you washed yourself again", and I told her "But we went to the toilet together last night", she said "No, I did not, you were probably dreaming", then my aunt washed me again and made me wear my clothes.

My grandmother and aunt-in-law were already in the stable, when we got up. They would deal with cows first. And then we would make our breakfast. Everyone was dealing with something. Then my grandmother came to me with a bucket, and a tray filled with breads. She told me "Now we are going somewhere, but it's a secret, so you shouldn't tell anyone about it", and I told her, "Okay, but where are we going grandma?", she said "We are going to go together for a while, then you need to walk alone, understood?", and I told her again "Okay grandma, but where are we going?", she finally said "We are going to a house, where there is a child just like you, but hungry without any food, understood?", then I realised and said "Oh". We started walking, we walked behind the house, on the cross sections of the fields. She told me to walk from a certain way not to cover my food in mud. Then she again reminded me our little secret. "We are going together just a for a while, then you need to go yourself, okay?", and I answered "Okay grandma, I'll go myself". We were at the edge of a field, and we stopped. She gave me the bread and the bucket. Bread was on my back, and in my hands, there was bucket filled with yogurt... "You just walk slowly; you need to go to the third house from this direction". I started walking, but also was looking behind to my grandma, she was also looking at me. Then I found the place.

Some kids opened the door, and they were surprised to see me. They welcomed into their home. I told them "My grandma told me to get back the tray and the bucket", they said to me "But our mother was not at home", just after their mother came back to their house. She was also surprised to see me. She came close to me and hugged. She was kissing me while patting my head.

"Whom did you come with?"

"I am alone."

"How did you come?"

"I came with grandma, she let me came here half way there. She said that you may not have any bread left", their mother was really affected by my words, and told me "Yes, we don't have any". Before I left, they started to organized the table. One the girls told her mother "We probably eat it at one sit, shouldn't we ask for another one from grandmother?", and then I told the girl "She is my grandmother, not yours". Then their mother came with me to the door. My grandmother was waiting a little ahead of the road. But the woman was like avoiding my grandmother. Anyway, I came next to my grandmother. I told her what happened, while we were walking towards our house. They never spoke to each other. My grandma told me "So they need two, okay then you should go to your mother to take another one. If you can find it there, you should take it back to that home". After that I went straight to our house. I asked my older sister. She said "Do you know that house?", I told her "Yes, of course I do". She told me what I was looking, and said "For bread". She said "We got no bread". We really didn't have any bread left. Then I started to play at garden a bit. But then I realised that I needed to get a bread. I couldn't wait there, went to my grandfather's, and

I took one bread from the cabinet. Then from time to time, I would start to go there to take some bread with me. I was calling the woman "sister", but one of the boys from neighbourhood told me that I shouldn't have called him sister. I was surprised to hear that. I asked why, he told me "Because she's your aunt". I was really surprised, so she was the sister of my father! Then I went right next to her and asked her "Is it true?", she said "Yes, I'm your aunt". And of course, her children were my cousins. So, in the end I realised that my aunt was not permitted to talk with any members of the family... She was married without the consent of her family. And my grandfather was angry at her. But he did not warn me about getting there and hanging out with them. Out of nowhere, I had friends, and they were my cousins...

One day, when my grandfather was pretty happy, I told him "Grandpa, I'm really sad about the situation of my aunt. You are angry at her because they are poor", he then told me "It's normally none of a child's business, but it seems like you got the wrong impression. So, let me clarify for you; I'm not mad at her because she married some poor guy. I'm mad at her, because she married with an engaged man. Maybe she was thoughtless, I don't know. But it's something that's easy to forget. Yes, she is my daughter, and will always be. But also, I will always be angry towards her". But of course, he was really affected because of this conversation. The important thing here is that he said everything to me, to let me know and teach me a lesson about a misfortunate event. Like some part of an education that comes from family... If he had just got angry because of my questions, I would probably haven't been able to understood what he had felt.

Of course, people always make choices. And they make those choice for their own happiness. Also, not always the little ones are the one who are mistaken. Older people could also be at wrong sometimes. They would usually say, you shouldn't go to school, instead you could be a tailor, or they would just decide who to marry their daughter, on behalf of her name, or simply wouldn't let a girl go to the school, just because she's a girl. And mostly, people would marry the ones who was chosen by their parents. And if something bad had happened, older people would just have told them "That's just your destiny". Which is the destiny? Is it when people choose by their own, or is it when things got decided by someone else?

One day, my grandfather let me sit on his lap, and told me "You will be a grown-up in a brief time. You will start your own life. You should consider all those things, and decide all by yourself. You should be careful. You should always put family front, you should be respectful toward principles of your family, even though they might be wrong from time to time. But you should always have your respect. Because sometimes you might think, you are completely right, but time will fly away you will realise actually they were right all along. The right decision was always taken with the consent of your family. Because, us, the older people, come together to speak a matter, even about its little perspective. If it's right for family, we don't stay in front of it. Thus, everyone will be happy this way". I wish everything would be this easy and perfect... But unfortunately, not everyone this civil. Everyone can grow up, but only can be mature, and unfortunately not everyone is entitled to be right.

And of course, youngsters are always regarded as disrespectful. But are they treating older people just because they are disrespectful, or are they fed up with the nonsenses...? We all have problems. But the important thing is to found out the power of trust, love, respect, all those important aspects of life that we lost. I always wish that we would respect both family and the person, wish we would have the respect towards each other... Yes, we cannot expect everyone to be right, trustful or respectful, but we, at least, expect our family members to be right, respectful or trustful. So that, we can build something important within the family, if there's fairness within a family, if every member of the family respects each other, their thought, and beliefs. If all those present inside a family, then a member of that family can be self-confident, and solid. And there would not be any need of deceiving, or deluding. The unity of a family can gets stronger with a good communication. In the old times, the greatest task for a woman was to become a good wife. Girls were having dreams of a good marriage. Because there was no other option for them. Even if there is a small chance, they didn't have the courage to take that risk. So, the main goal was to get married, have stable life. If your husband was poor, then you would live a poor life, if he is rich, then you would way more comfortable. At least, you have some food not to stay hungry. Any assurance for yourself? None. People back then knew nothing about getting retired. They would always want to work. But if you cannot work? Back in time women would say, my children would take care of me. How can someone feel happy, trapped inside this kind of world? Maybe they were under hard conditions, but that was the only thing on their hands. There were patient people, who looked after their old ones, but there were also some people, that told them why don't you die...

During a conversation, my grandfather told me;

"So, you can read now, and you can also write letters. So, tell me, what do you want to be in the future?"

"What do you mean, I'm just reading."

"Yes, people read. But they do it to get a profession. Such as teachers, doctors, nurses... What do you want to be?"

"Grandpa, I have never thought about it before. What do you think?"

"I will be old when you grow up, so you should be a doctor. At least, you can take care of me."

"Oh, that is great! Yes, I will become a doctor, and take care of you!"

"Okay, then that's a deal!"

"Yes, a deal!"

This little talk with my grandpa was serious for me. From now on, I had a goal.

The roads leading us to the school were terrible. My grandfather submitted a petition to the directorate of highways, and they started the construction later. Some were happy about it, but there were also some envy faces... Thanks to the construction, now we had even more opportunity to go and come back from school even though it was done with a tractor. It was even fine for us to walk, because there were pebble stones on the ground, and not mud just like before. This was a total ease for us. People were grateful, because this was a service for us all. School, work, shopping... It was necessary for all needs.

If there was any problem concerning the village, people would always come to seek my grandfather. Almost everyone would want to have his moral support. Like a fight over a land, or two lovers who wanted to get married, or families that are angry towards each other, or asking for a girl in marriage... My grandfather was the only one between his peers that knew two languages -Greek and Turkish- and can read Quran in Arabic and translate it, so he was educated.

When I got to know this side of my grandfather, I started ask questions about them. I once told him, "Grandpa, how did you learn to speak Greek?", he started to tell me his history. He was born in Batumi, in Georgia. His father, Hüseyin, went to the Georgia, when Ottoman Empire still ruling there, and bought a land to work and live on it. After the death of his first wife, he got married with Rukiye, my grandfather's mother, and went to the Batumi from Trabzon Çaykara. They were producing crops, tobacco, and corn. They knew the details of corn farming, but have almost no clue about crops or tobacco. They thought, they got to know it along the way. During this time, great-grandmother Rukiye got pregnant. They were using the same water-channel with the field just across the creek. My great-grandfather's field was on right side of the hill, and the field across the creek was on the other hill, between them there was a beautiful creek, and right next to it a water-well for them. My great-grandfather told my great-grandmother to go with the worker, for her safety. He asked her to go to the field across the creek.

So, great-grandmother Rukiye was walking, when she saw the lady on the next field. They greeted each other. The lady told her "So, you are new at this job. Where are you from?", my great-grandmother said "From Türkiye. We are new here, and have no one else, but we got a huge field, even though we do not have that much knowledge about it," then the lady said "Whom did you came with? Are you married, or are you with your family?" my great-grandmother told her "Yes, I'm married, I'm with my husband, and those are our workers". Meriam was the name of that lady, she told her "I wish you a happy life, so, how's it going for you, everything well?" Granny Rukiye said "Yes, we are fine, but I've missed my family. I have never been out till this day; I was bored too much. Also, I am pregnant, it has been three months. And I have no one to share with." After this sentence, Meriam told her "Well I am pregnant too, and that is my third time. The first two are dead now, unfortunately. But I am well-experienced with it now. If it is okay for you, I could be your sister, and help you through your pregnancy." And Granny Rukiye asked her "Why did they die?" she told her "My breast milk is toxic. I cannot give it to my child, in my first two try, both are died because of this reason. That is the third time, so we are thinking about another option."

Then Granny Rukiye told her "Well you said you could be my sister, so I could do something in return. I could breastfeed your child, so that he could live. And you could breastfeed my child, so that we will have no problem at all", Merriam was happy; "Well, that would be terrific! But we are Jew. If that is okay for you, we could work it out, and it would be the best present I have ever gotten in my life".

So, they calculated the date of the possible births. They realised, it is the same month, and even the same day. This coincidence created a friendship between two families. That

Jew family, helped my great-grandfather almost about anything. They showed them how to produce crops or tobacco. And then the day came; both ladies gave birth that day, one in the morning, on at night... They both had a boy, and as they had talked before, they took the children of one another for breastfeeding. Two boys grew up as health as possible for a human being. Four years later, Granny Rukiye had another boy, a brother for my grandfather. Then my grandfather went to the school. During those days, alphabet of Turkish language was Arabic. And the mostly spoken language was Greek. All trade works and social interactions was done via Greek language. So, my grandfather and his family cared about this matter, they learned how to speak Greek, and their Greek neighbours also learned Turkish. So, spoken languages of that region was Greek and Turkish. They had a bit hard time, when they were trying to speak with Russians, but when it came to the Greek or Turkish, things were perfect for them. They lived there happily for ten years. They had couple of caretakers, many different workers, and had strong relations with the folk around... My grandfather once told me "Those ten years were there richest and greatest year of our life."

And just couple of years later; some grossing politics destroyed the friendships. The war came... Main problem for my grandfather and his family was their nationality. They were Turks. They had two options, whether they would change their religion to Christianity, or die. But they had another option, trying to flee to Türkiye. From then on, The Great War was supressing the whole world.

Russian soldiers were looking for my grandfather. They were looking him, because they wanted to send him to the Siberia.

Those times Siberia were impossible to live on. People were telling stories about how even the breath of a man just get frozen. In the end, it meant freezing to death. So, my great-grandfather chose to flee. But then soldier came to the house, and they were looking for him. Grandpa Hüseyin decided to wear the clothes of his wife, pretending to be a woman. Then soldiers came to the house and asked my great-grandmother "Where is Hüseyin?" she told them "He fled. What do you think? Would ever a man who is afraid of death, stay in this house?", and they asked "Then who is this old woman?", she told "She's my mother, when she heard Hüseyin fled, she came to our house to help me". So, that was how my great-grandfather managed to flee. Soldiers took everything from them, their house, money, valuable items... They were left with nothing. They have lived under the threat of death for four years. For those four years, that Jew family helped them to live a proper life, by selling my great-grandfathers goods like it was his. And one day, when things got calm a bit, they decided to flee. They fled with a small sailing boat. They hopped on it at night, and managed to get to Türkiye in the morning. They first went to the Bayburt. Then my great-grandfather went to his homeland, Çaykara, Trabzon. He went there with nothing in his pockets. So, he tried to work some quick job, to help his own family. At the meantime, he was looking for a land to settle. Then he bought a new land, even though it was not as big as it was in Georgia.

My grandfather was sixteen, and his brother was eight when they had decided to settle in Bafta. In Bafra, there had been many Greeks back in time. But Atatürk had a deal with Greek government, and sent them to their home country; Greece, and Turks that was living in Greece came back to Türkiye. So, there were many different people in our village, that came from all different cities and countries; people from Albania, from Salonica. And people from Trabzon; they were called Laz people. And still you can find all these people that came from different countries in our village (Back in time, people from Trabzon were called as Laz, even though many of them were not Laz).

Our village was designed for Turks. But not everyone was okay with it. During my childhood, people were still distant from each other. Problems of the history, made people to act distantly. There were still fear and worry.

And during my childhood, there was also a war in Cyprus in the year 1974. People in Bafra were scared, because they thought there would be another occupation, or civil war. They afraid that people would get killed.

My grandfather's education was halted as a result of the occupation. And, things were not great in Türkiye either, so many people stopped their education journey. Many even did not have a chance to think about education, mainly because they were trying to survive, and many did not choice the option of education, just because economic reasons. Many people, including me during my childhood, were not be able to get a proper education. Political clashes between rightist, and leftist... In our country, there always has been political problems. People cannot express their own feeling and ideas, even during just a regular visit to their neighbours. Our society is not ready for such freedom. I do not know, whether it is because of laws or not, but people are not that open to the different ideas. So, thanks to that, people can get angry at each other, even there is not any proper reason. For example; people just focus on the surface. They just look at an institution, or a person and only think about in shallowly. And this problem leads people into mistakes. In order to understand a person properly, you need to get familiar with him. If you do not have this as an option, it is the best not to talk about that person at all.

You do not need to think about a person, just because you want to think him/her like that. You should not try to dishonour a person just because he is right, or fair. You cannot feel right, if you are doing this. This form of social illness, make us more distant every day. It eats trust and love, it even making the characteristic of a person toxic.

If you want to have right decision, then you should think about it properly. And in order to manage that, people should be in peace with their own characteristic, and their life. If they are not that in peace with themselves, the only option for happiness is those people themselves. So, they should focus on the options that could make them happy. If the people are well developed, they can enjoy listening other people, to learn about their ideas and feelings. Being this open, just does not mean changing your religion, or your identity. It just an opportunity to discover different aspects of other people, and prevent the use of your personal aspects. It is a protection for yourself and your family. For example, Quran is one and only, but its interpretation is different in many aspects. Sometimes, people with bad intentions, try to target the beliefs of other people. Nowadays, many people know how to read and write, they are literate, so they had many options to properly develop themselves. Quran is the main resource leading us to a proper life and the afterlife. And the main mistake about this thing is; people trying to prayer in Arabic, just because they think it's a good deed, but in reality, we should read it in the way, we can understand, in our own language.

Allah has the comprehension of all languages on the face of the world. Allah can hear our prayers, regardless of which language they had been done. The important thing is; what do we understand from the things we read?

Family Relations

Our father was at Germany. My mother, and my other siblings were living on the house that my father helped it was done. I, on the other hand, was on the house of my grandfather, with my grandma and grandpa. My uncles, aunt-in-laws and aunt were telling me to go to the other house, to see my brothers. But they did not want me in their house. They told me not to come there, and even tried to beat me. So, I have never been there. My mother, on the other hand, has never loved me. When my brothers beat me for no proper reason, she would do nothing. So, I would go back to my grandfather's. And my aunts, and uncles would ask me all the time "Why did you come back?" and I would tell them what happen. But my grandfather never insisted to me to go there.

Sometimes, my mother would call me to help her for writing a letter to my father, or when she would go shopping to help her with money. I would go to help her every time, but there was always a tension between us. I had a sense inside me, telling me that I did not love her. She was not the mother for me... I would miss my mother, and cried about it to my grandma. My grandma would try to divert me from those bad feeling, and tell me to go play with my friends. I would go to the garden, to my aunt's place to play with other kids. Neighbours would always smile at me. I would stay a bit, and play. And then it was my time to go back. On the way back, I would go to my grandfathers again.

My grandfather, and father of my aunt-in-law Bahattin Uncle would meet regularly. They had long talked about past... During those talks many common ideas were spoken; you can be mistaken, but it's important to correct your mistake, try to stay right, you shouldn't act wrong, you should be a decent person, ignorance is the result of wrong actions, happiness is the result of good deeds, may Allah help our kids... Bahattin Uncle would tell jokes; "Well, those are our good days, in the future we wouldn't be able to find people to talk about those things".

On day, my grandfather called my aunt and told her;

"Maka my granddaughter ready, I will take her to the centre."

My aunt said;

"Well, your granddaughter is like gold dust. Now she is going to the centre, eh?"

"Yes, I will take her of course. I will take her many books, so that she will read them and become a doctor in the future."

In our previous talks, we shared an opinion on, me being a doctor. But I did not even know what a doctor is, so I asked;

"Grandpa, what is a doctor?"

He told me;

"A doctor cures the patients and ill people. She would prescribe relevant medications to them, so that they take it and be better."

I was just a little kid, and I did not know anything about doctors. I had never seen a doctor back then. I learned a new profession this way, well it was new to me at least. Because there was no doctor at our village, we had no hospital, health centre, or dispensary. If you felt sick, you would go to the Samsun or Bafra back in time.

It was the next day, and my aunt made my prettiest clothes ready. I had a beautiful red dress, red shoes, white socks, and a green coat with white furs. There were pompons on my shoes. They were white and soft. I would always play with them, because I always thought they were soft and funny.

We were ready to go to the centre. My grandpa had his black fedora, and black coat on him. He also put his famous perfume on. He would always like to look after himself. There was almost no car on the road just ahead of our house. So, we walked towards the main road for almost 15 minutes. Then we hopped on a bus. We greeted everyone in the bus, and had a daily conversation. They saw me next to my grandpa, and asked him "Is there something wrong with your granddaughter İzzet? She seems fine." My grandpa told them;

"No, no. She had no problem thanks to God. She even does not know what a doctor is. We are just going to take a walk at the centre."

Everyone was a bit shocked, because it was an uncommon situation. Showing your affection directly to your granddaughter, taking her outside; those were uncommon... I was too happy, and did not even realise there was something wrong. As I grew up, I understood that my grandpa and my grandma was always onto me. When people asked my grandma about why I did not hang out with my mother but with them, she would simply say; "She is the only girl of these two houses. We like having her in our house."

That was a great answer, but in the other house; I had got no one to share with. Even though many people were fond of me, my brothers were always distant at me. I was asking why? Why my own mother did not even care about me, when my brothers kicked me, a little girl, out of house in the middle of a night? I was getting kicked out of my own house, and when I went to the other one, they were telling me to go back, to make things easy with me and my brothers... I was so scared of them, I was telling my aunt "Aunt, please come with me". As I grew up, things started to change. I had problems while I was expressing myself. They were still insisting about me getting back to my house, and the only thing I did was to cry it over to my grandpa and my grandma.

My grandpa would always buy me story books, and I read them with a great desire. I would dream about being the main character of the story. I would change the parts that I did not like. I would dream them however they made me feel funny. Sometimes my grandpa would gather us around him. Once he taught us how to play horon. And sometimes he would tell us good stories. But those good moments were temporarily. Just a second later, fighting with my brothers would start again, and that woman I called as my mother would do nothing about it as always.

My grandpa and grandma would always insist my mother about showing me some affection. Once my grandpa told her "If you want to have your husband back, this child is the only option. You should take care of her, so that you can have him back." I did not understand why he said that. After this weird talk, my mother once told me "Girl, come here, let's eat together". There was also my sister. My sister would always be nice to me. I looked at her. She was smiling, so, I went and sat with them. It was lunch, and the meal was leaf lettuce. My mother took a piece of bread and filled it with the meal, she then put it into my mouth and said "Open your mouth, eat it." I opened my mouth, and swallowed it. But the moment I swallowed it, I started running to toilet. It was gross. There were hair strands inside it. I felt disgusted. My sister was shocked, she said "Oh no mother, she's going to die!" I exited the toiled and told my sister "I'm fine, I threw up", but I was so angry. My sister said "Do you want to eat again?" I told her "No, I'm full!", my mother found these words funny. Then I went straight to my grandma. I told her what happened. She got angry, and told me "That's it, I'm going to send it to your father", I asked in surprised "But my father is working there, what will I do all alone at home?", she said "I will send you to your mother". I did not understand it, "My mother? Isn't that lady my mother?" she said "No, she's not your mother." I was both surprised and happy. From that day on I was telling everyone "I'm going to my mum!"

One day, we went to a wedding. I also talked about it to my peers. My mother heard it, and complained me to my aunt. My aunt came towards me and slapped me on my mouth hard. That happened, when I was with my friends.

"I will never hear those words again out of your mouth. She is your mother; you have no mother elsewhere. So, stop lying everyone. If you say those words again, I will beat you up!" she said.

I was angry and looked at her. But I could not do anything. I went straight to home, and told what happened to my grandma. My grandma said "Okay, do not you worry. When your father comes back, I will send you with him. You just wait in patience", and I replied "Okay!".

I was reading the stories that my grandpa bought me one by one. In the meantime, I was also studying my homework. One day, my grandpa asked some question about the stories, to figure out whether I read them or not. So, I started to explain the stories to my grandpa. I would read the stories out loud, that was the only way for me to understood them well.

My grandpa would tell me about the animals that were in the stories. For example, cats would be ungrateful towards their owners, you feed them and make them grow up, but they would not feel grateful. Dogs, on the other hand, are the friends of people. They would be grateful towards their owners; they would try their best to protect them. We had many cows back then. So, I asked about them, he said "Their owners know them well. They do not protect their owners, but they are sacred animals. They feed us with their milk, and meat.", and for horses he said "We can't eat their meat. But it has been told that, you can eat their right side, if you are in hunger. They are noble creatures. They always stick with you, no matter what. They are also smart."

I would share everything I learned from reading with my friends on the way to school. One day, on the way to home from school, I fell. I was covered with mud; my coat was also in mud. I said "Oh no, I fell! I got covered in mud, look!" and my friend pretended to be helping, but made things worse. Because my friend never had any coat, or shoes like mine. He was jealous of me. I was sad because my coat and actions of my friend. I got angry, and never talked with my friend, I said "Don't touch me ever again!"

I was on good terms with my friends. I was not even aware of my clothes. It was good for our health to wear a proper coat on winters, but some only had a sweater, and some did not even have any. Some families were living really under bad conditions, and other were just thoughtless.

Next, they bought me new shoes, they got me the same shoes with my siblings. Rubber shoes, etc... One day, I had a rehearsal for 23rd April show. I had a choir dress with puff sleeves. In order to properly wore it, I needed to wear a short underwear. There was almost a war at home. My brother took my underwear and wore it, and I could not do anything to prevent him. What is left for me was a long underwear. I wore it, and went to the rehearsal. But lower parts of the long underwear could be seen under my dress. My teacher saw it, and said "What kind of underwear is that?" and I told her "It's my brother's". My teacher said "Look at her! Answering me!" I was really embarrassed. If kids are left alone on these kinds of problems, nothing can be done properly.

I was ashamed of what happened. That is why I didn't go to school. My grandma bathed me, and made me wear red underwear, and told me "Now, let's go and play with your siblings!", I ran towards my brothers and sisters. But my older brother came towards me with anger, and pricked a tobacco needle to me. I passed out that exact moment. When I woke up, my leg was covered with bandage, and there were many people who came to see me.

During these kinds of problems, adults should be the competent ones to prevent these to happen. I was raised with a great interest from my grandpa and grandma, so, when other kids were jealous of me, they would simply tell lies. Of course, I was the targets of those lies, and sometimes violence.

I do not know exactly, whether the parents of those kids were satisfied with their kids back then, but they were silence towards those actions (telling lies, stealing, etc.), and that let those kids to be the sneaky, prick, hypocrite, and damaging people that we see today. You should be blind not to see those people and not to believe that all the problems are just the result of their childhood period.

Personal development is a huge concern. In some parts of Türkiye, people do not respect others as a human being, and as an individual. People still have strict lines. Of course, there are still hard-headed thoughts, like; you need to be married in order to get along with others, or you cannot get married if you have already passed an age... Yes, marriage is a good thing for a human being. People need to get into the marriage by their own consent; so that they can build a family which is safe and peaceful, they can bring up children in peace, they can let children know that they are being loved, they can create good individuals for the society... Being a father, or a mother is the easiest part, but having the ability to share some time with your own kid is the actual struggle.

There are thousands of short-tempered kids around the globe. The reason of them being short-tempered, is the lack of love and attention. A child needs to fell that love from the time he/she was born, till his/her adulthood. There are many different traditions in Europe about personal development. For example, when a kid turns 18, he/she can leave his/her house, that is even happening when they turn 16. I think, this is also a problematic custom.

The right way to do this; is to find the perfect moment, that the person is completed educationally, physically, and emotionally. We should make our kids ready to this process with education, but not with pressure. And when you decide to get marry, you should be ready for that kind of a responsibility.

There might be problems in a marriage, even if it was done as a result of a love. As an addition, there could be no marriage in the face of the world that is completely perfect. But if a couple try their best to solve their problems, then we can say that, this is a well-adjusted couple. And if there's happiness, respect, trust, and honesty, we can completely say that, it is a successful marriage. Sharing a home together is completely different than being in love with that person. The expectations are normally; love, respect, trust, ability to talk over problems, and sharing. And those are not just the expectations of a marriage, but for everything in life; friendship, relation of a child and his/her mother...

Let us analyse together: How many friends do you have that you can say I trust him/her completely? When I asked this question to the people around me, the answers are always the same. They either say none, or just a couple, not much. What do you think about reason behind this? According to my experiences; I do not think there are many couple who focus on the expectations that I mentioned above before having a child. If there is any, I congratulate them with honesty. Also, we can see that; people are just unhappy, they want to divorce, some are just trying to make things work by on their own, and even there are people who want to have child, just because not to let another person go away. As you can understand; children are always in the background. People are literally using children as a shield for themselves in marriages. But those people seem to forget something. Children always want to be the first, they want to get the attention they need from their parents. They are aware of almost everything. They face with untruthfulness in the first years of their life, and even by the hands of their parents. I need to add something here: Which one is more important? Doing almost everything to work out a marriage for just not to stay alone, or the sanity of the children?

The mortal world is filled with sudden deaths. People might lose their partners, and face with the hardship of being alone in the world. And, this is not that rare. There might be a sudden break-up. If a person decides to head out to the wilderness of the world with his/her child, he/she need have a proper financial capability, and he/she need to spend his/her life for happiness. The proper way to do this comes from a good education and a nice profession.

When we compare Turkish society with European societies, we can see that, there are less kids in Western societies, because they mostly focus on their own education. Even a person is married, he/she continues his/her education. It is a healthy action to make yourself ready to life through education, not only for people, but also for their beloved ones. This way, one can improve his/her self-confidence, and crate a stronger person. We just need to be a little bit brave and hardworking. In this way, we, for sure, can create a better life for ourselves. When do people feel happy? When they see their beloved ones in happy, and healthy conditions...

We might have been raised properly by our parents, but that is not a hinder in our path to raise our children better. With all goodness and badness, every moment we have lived is an experience for us. We can create a better future, if we focus on the effort to give better, and right conditions to our children.

We should always remember; a properly raised child, is an investment to the future for our society. We should always remind our children with examples that; telling lies, and trying to deceive others are just temporary options. When we are having a conversation with them, we should make them feel loved, and deemed important. We should not talk with them like getting a report from them. If you just make a small effort to understand them, and reply them with interest, you can easily spot the difference on them. You can be closer this way, and you can see the interest by your children. In the end, all these efforts, will create a moral strength both for you and your children, and you will be in peace.

Our Beloved Ones

It was just like other days. Summer had already passed through, and it was time for winter. My grandma's family was residing in Samsun, and she would go there regularly every winter. So, I would go with her all the time. And this time, she decided to go without me. She told me "This time you can't come, because you have a school to go", so I said "Okay". Then she went there to see her family, and I went to my father's house to stay with my brothers, because we were going to school together. That day, we were getting ready for school, then someone knocked the door. We opened it, there was our cousin Cengiz outside. We were really surprised to see him, so we asked "What happened?".

He told us "I've bad news. My aunt passed away last night; we brought her body for funeral". We were shocked. My grandma passed away. Her death created a hole inside me. I was devastated about it. That was the first funeral I attended in my life. Funeral of my lovely grandma, who I had spent time with, I love so much... She was gone now. I went straight to my grandpa's. I could not believe it.

I told them "Show her to me!" then they showed me her face. She was just lying there. I felt so weird and bad. Then they gave me a task to accomplish. They told me to tell the news to my aunt that was staying that other house. My grandma's brother said:

"You know her house. So, you should go and tell her to come to see her mother one last time."

So, I was crying, and running to my aunt's house. When I got there, I realised she had already gotten the news. She was running around the house while crying. She did not know what to do. I called her name twice; "Aunt!"

"What happened?"

"I came here to take you back to my grandpa's. My grandma is dead, we need to go there now."

"Okay, let's go then" she said.

That was how my aunt came back to his parents' house after 8 years. Everyone was shocked because of this sudden death, and of course, we had nothing to do. It was destiny. They told me she died because of a heart attack. The funeral had been done, and we paid our last respects. From then on, I had two holes inside me, and I showed them by writing two names on fogged windows: grandma and mum.

As a result of the destiny, my grandma, who told me that she would send me to Germany to my father, was gone now. I was sad, and the bad thing was that, I could not talk about the matters on my mother with no one. They gave me no chance to talk on that matter.

Death of my grandma… I do not know, maybe it was a direct result of a sudden death, but people around me started to treat me fairly… My aunt started to visit us regularly. Me, and my brothers, and my sister was getting closer as siblings, during my visit on their house.

Two, or three months later, my grandpa told us "Only God is solitude. I am going to find a lady, and marry her", and so he did. He found a woman from his hometown Çaykara. After a couple days

of his marriage, he told me "She is not your real grandma, I know that. But your grandma is gone now. You should treat her fair, so that she does the same in return, and we all can be happy."

Then he asked "Do we have a deal my granddaughter?" I was thinking "Yes, my grandma is death now, and my grandpa is married. It is soon or later," and told my grandpa "Yes, we have a deal". Yes, we had a deal as granddaughter and grandfather, but not everyone was happy with the decision of my grandpa. The bitter pain that comes from the sudden death of my grandma was still around. People was thinking that my grandpa was a bit early to marry another woman, in the end it was just a little time. So, they were a bit uncomfortable with it. Especially my aunts and uncles… But no one said anything wrong, or had a fight with my grandpa. They said, the thing is done. There was a common rule about not asking why to the older people, because it was considered that they knew the best, so there was always respect towards older people.

Of course, my father was not with us. He was at Germany. He even did not know about his mother's death. He was there, working as a worker. Back in those times, he could not come here to visit us regularly. After a little later, my grandpa talked about it to my father. There were only two options for communication. One was letter, which was the slowest way, and the other was telegraph, which was only used for urgent matters. And, at best, we would send a letter per one, or two weeks. We would always try our best to keep communication good. And one day, we found out that my grandpa had taken new decisions. This time it was about my uncles. He wanted them to marry, and my father told my grandpa that he had a good friend called Cemil, and Cemil had a girl, that they could try their chance with. My father said he would be happy to see them together another arrange marriage.

First, my grandpa spoke with my uncles, whether they were thinking about someone or not. He did not consider my older uncle's decision appropriate, but gave permission to my younger uncle. So, they had talks with the girl's family, about a possible marriage to my younger uncle. But that family said no. Then my grandpa decided to marry my younger uncle to Nergiz who was a relative to my grandma. For my older uncle, he thought that my father's friend Cemil's daughter would be a good option. So, it was time to meet with other families.

Meanwhile, my mother was angry at my grandpa. She said "I am married too, and I have five children, my husband should come back here." I could not hear my grandpa's answer to her, because they took me outside. When I came back at home later that night, my mother was fuming. She pointed at me and said

"He left his child with me, and went away". My mother was angry towards me, just like my brothers, but they would even beat me from time to time. So, the action was on. My mother told the same thing to my grandpa a couple of times. This made everyone uncomfortable. But of course, I could not witness any of those talks. I was just a kid, and only was aware of some stuff. I still needed to grow up to understand why, and realised the true meanings of problems.

And the good news... After his mother's sudden death, my father decided to take a break from work, and came back here. My grandma had always waited for her son, but could not see him. Just like my father... When I first saw him, I started running towards him. He hugged me, and we started walking to my grandpa's. Our neighbour Uncle Bahattin was also with us. I told my father "Dad, I can walk, I grew up!" Uncle Bahattin said the same thing, "Yes, she can walk, she's a young girl now."

There was a mourning again in the house when my father came back. But then we had a talk about family matters. Then, we found a car, and went to the house of my father's friend Cemil. My father did not stay that long, and went straight back to Germany. And of course, no one asked anything to my older uncle, whether he wanted to marry that girl or not. My grandpa took the decisive decision, and the rest was just procedures. And sometime later, there was a candidate for my aunt also.

My aunt's marriage was done even before both of my uncles.' For both of my uncle, we made a ceremony of binding with a promise to wed. We declared that to everyone in our village by firing guns.

My uncle's wife's house was close to my school. One day she saw me and told me;

"Hey, Hüsniye,"

"Yes aunt?"

"We talked with your uncle. There is a long distance to your house from there. You can stay with me this weekend,"

"That's great to hear aunt, but I'm okay with walking down to my house with my friends,"

"If so, you just stay this night then?"

"Not this night. I cannot. But let me ask my mother, maybe I will come tomorrow." She just said "Okay," I had Melek right next to me. She was the daughter of my aunt.

Melek was making fun of me while we were walking. She told me, while she was laughing;

"Your aunt cares about you."

"So? She is going to marry with my uncle."

I think, she was just a bit jealous of me.

I told her, "So what? I also care about you, so you can stay with me tonight, if you want?" We had a good laugh. So, she decided to stay at our house that night. We went to our house. We had our dinner, we studied our homework, and spent time a bit. Next morning, we got up, and went straight to the school. After that school day, we were on our way to our houses. But then I realised, I forgot to ask my mother about staying with my aunt! And my aunt was also waiting for me. I got excited. I told Melek "I can go straight to my aunt and tell her about what happened," but she told me "Don't worry, you just go straight to your aunt's, I'll tell your mother." But I was not so sure about that. I thought she would not probably tell my mother anything.

So, I told her, "No, don't wait for me, I could just go straight to my aunt, and tell her about it."

I had a distress within me. Like a voice inside me was telling me to go there. And it would be disgraceful not to go to my aunt's. So, I went to my aunt's running, and tried to explain what happened to my aunt. My aunt, also, got panicky. Because it was getting dark out there. She told me "Wait, I'll go with you." While we were having this conversation, a bus just got passed there. My aunt opened his garden door to take me down the road, but it was all foggy! She was trying to find a good path to take me. But then we saw an old lady in the woods. She also seemed lost, but she was on a field.

My aunt recognised her immediately. She said "Hey, that's my aunt!" I asked "Which one?", she said "Aunt Gülperi". Aunt Gülperi was my father's aunt. She was old, and her sight was not in perfect conditions. And even under these foggy conditions... My aunt told me "Go, watch out for her Hüsniye, she seems lost," I said "Okay aunt," and went straight to her. I called her "Aunt!" she did not recognise me and asked "Where am I? That dirty dog left me middle of nowhere!" She was also crying. I told her "Aunt, it's me," she said "Who are you?"

"Aunt! It is me Hüsniye."

"Oh, Hüsniye, is that you? What are you doing here?

"Never mind aunt, just give me your bag. Let me just take you to the edge of the field, so that you can walk properly. Come, give me your hand, lets walk together, and have some talk. Do not worry, I will take you home."

"Oh, okay, but the man left me here, told me I can go from here, I don't know who he was."

My dear aunt was scared, I told her "Aunt, don't worry, you're on a field, now I'm going to take you on road, so that we can walk there."

"Now, where are we going my sweet girl?"

"I am taking you to our house. Once we get there, we will do the rest."

"Oh, okay then. That would be enough for me."

We walked to our house at a slow pace, so that my aunt would not be uncomfortable. People back at our house were surprised to see us. My aunt was covered in mud. We made the water ready, and bathed her. Then I had a bath. We had our dinner. But, Aunt Gülperi was staying with the son of my father's uncle. And my aunt was also married with her uncle's son, so Aunt Gülperi was staying with them. Their house was at a distant place, it would take almost thirty minutes to go there... Of course, there was no phone, so we could not notify anyone. But then, my aunt's husband got curious about Aunt Gülperi, took a bus, and started looking at every road in our village. Around ten at night, they knocked the door of Mikail, because they were thinking she might have gone there. So, we answered the door, Uncle Yusuf saw him first. He was ashen-faced. He said "Oh no, what did I do? My aunt went missing just because of me. I let her go with that man on the bus. She cannot survive this night, she will freeze to death!", but then he saw Aunt Gülperi. He was relieved. He said "Oh, thanks to God. I came here off chance, but there she is." Then he turned back to me and told me "Thank you my girl, you saved a life!"

He told us "I think she should stay here this night, she must be exhausted", then he was gone. We talked about this for a matter of time. After that day, Aunt Gülperi would hug me every time she saw me. The thing is, that man on the bus was our neighbour, but he left almost a blind lady in the middle of nowhere…

Our houses were on the same street. So, he needed to pass between our house and my aunt's house. He could have easily brought that old woman to us, but at least it did end well for us.

Seven months later, both of my uncles got married in the same wedding. There was no invitation in our village, everyone was invited automatically. We would only send invitations to the people in different cities. It was a very crowded wedding. Men had their fun with shawm-and-drum, and ladies had fun with gramophone and records. There were many records at my uncle's. But of course, the gramophone was powered with batteries, because there was no electricity. So, there was no problem for those who wanted to have fun. Those years a song called "Tin tin tinimini hanım" was very popular. So, women were dancing to that song. I seemed so much fun. When it was "tin tin" part, everyone would crouch, and then everyone would jump and dance in the "I love you" part of the song.

My both uncles had stayed together for a while. My grandpa had nine children; five girls, and four boys. So, those two uncles of mine were the last single ones. From then on, all my three uncles started to live in grandpa's.

One of my uncles, got married with Mahmure; the daughter of my father's friend Cemil. Things were quite normal till the wedding. Mahmure was a little weird, at least that was our thoughts. She was a stranger to this village, maybe that was the reason of her weirdness. Mahmure's mother also would come to us, to see her girl. One day, she wanted to talk with my mother. She told her "So you're Mikail's wife?", and my mother said "Yes", she then said "We know he got married there".

My mother pointed at me, and Mahmure shooed me away from that room, just like a cat, in my own house... So, I left there without saying anything.

Soon after, news was not great about my father. We learned that he got sick. In the meantime, Mahmure left the village, they went to Samsun with my uncle. My uncle would take me with him sometimes, to be a company to them. But Mahmure had never loved me, and that is way she would always be uncomfortable. I was on better terms with my other aunts Nergiz and Melehat. Problems inside the family were being reflected to us. Just like every other family, there were fights, as well as good times with sisters and brothers... I, still would go to my granpa's whenever a problem occurred.

There was news about my father's health condition. He underwent three operations. My mother, on the other hand, wanted him to come back. She never had any intentions about going to Germany.

One year later, my mother called me and my brothers, she told them; "From now on, you can't beat your sister, she's your sister", then they just said "Okay".

I had an exam in school during those years. It was an exam for student who want to study in a boarding public school. I won it, but I was too young to went there. Normally people would start elementary school at the age seven, but I started when I was four. And I was even younger in my identity card. My name was different too. In my identity, it was Hamiye. But everyone would call me "Hüsniye," even in school my teacher would take my attendance with my school number, but not with my name. When I asked about that, my grandpa told me "You are the younger of all your siblings. When your father applied for Germany, conditions was that an applicant could have maximum four children. That is why we registered you later, and changed your name". It did not take long, and my father came back here in the morning... I ran towards him and hugged him. My father was sad, and even his eyes filled with tears. Everyone came to say welcome. Whenever my father would come, there would be a holiday atmosphere in our home. He would always bring chocolates, candies. This time he came back permanently, we were going to live together. And from then on, we were going to do our real profession, in our own field; tobacco farming.

When my father came back, I was at fifth grade in elementary school. My uncle Helim was working in the accounting department of secondary school. In order to enrol me to the secondary school, a consent from my parents were necessary. My father was thinking about getting me to the school, but then he changed his mind and decided to take me from school. Now there were many rules' changes in the house. He forbade me from staying at someone else's house. He was not the same person that I wrote letters... He always saw me as a dog who wander around, or as extravagant with all my books and notebooks. I got no notebook left to do my homework, and that was a problem. I told about that problem to my teacher, and she got surprised too. She wanted to speak with my grandpa, and dad. My father's actions both hurt me and made me feel sad. And I also felt scared. I looked at my grandpa's eyes, and I was crying. I told them "What's going on?". I told the problem to my teacher, but nothing else. My father was looking at me in anger. I feared him. When we got back to home, I tried to avoid my father. I was trying to hide under the skirt of my sister. I got disappointed. There was a huge gap between me and my father... I was talking with my brother about what happened. I told them "He won't let me go to school." They said, "You need to be patient, he might change his mind." Later, I talked with my grandpa;

"Grandpa, do you know that my father will not let me go to school? He says a girl does not need to study, there is no good in it."

"You just wait my girl; I have not spoken with him yet. I will let you know, after we have a conversation..."

Of course, I was crying my eyes out. My grandpa, and teacher from my school tried to talk with my father. They told him "She'll have a very bright future ahead, you'll do a goodness for her, if you let her study", but no one managed to change his mind. My grandpa told me to speak with my mother. So, that I tried.

"Mother, nothing will change. There is a secondary school in our village. I will go there, just like the way I go to my school now, please convince my father. Do you know why he does not trust me?"

She looked at me;

"Your father said it once, and that is it. There could be no words on his words. So, you should better get ready for chores, he is not going to let you study, he will only let your brother study, that is it." I was only 9, but they were acting like I was an adult. She would always think that there could be a badness in everyone, and she also tried to plant that inside us, both me and my brothers... When I talked about her actions to my aunt, she said "Well she is what she is. She has been like that forever, there is nothing to do, she is your mother."

And my grandpa told me "My beautiful girl, I am just a farmer, and I cannot earn that much. If I had that opportunity, I would send you to the secondary school." I complained about my mother to my grandpa, my aunts, and my older uncle; "She is not like my mother. We are always having problems with her. She never listens me, nor helps me. I do not know what to do now. I just want to study." Then Aunt Nergiz came up with an idea.

"You know what?"

"What?"

One of my uncles never had children. He was an accountant at school, and had a proper earning.

"Come with us. Be the children of my brother. Just be their girl, they will protect you", Aunt Melihat said nothing, but she nodded. I told my Aunt Nergiz, "Okay, talk with my uncles, so that he can talk with my father."

Couple of days later, I found out that my father was not okay with it. He told my uncle and grandpa "I won't let her go, she's, my daughter." He was always angry. He was having arguments with almost everyone, and my mother was complaining about almost everyone. He argued with my grandpa, and my grandpa's brother, his uncle. Problems were fields and money...

I was not close with my father anymore. It was summer, and it was time to work. All of us, as siblings, started to work. Tobacco, corn, crops... All of us worked so hard that summer. We shared our responsibilities. We, all, were hard workers. But my father was filled with stress. He was smoking two pack in a day. He even started to beat my mother, when he just got stressed. In the meantime, as siblings, we decided to intervene. One day, when my father was beating my mother as usual, I called my brothers. They came inside, and told my father:

"Do not beat mum. If you ever touch her again, you will find us! We do not know whatever your problem is, but solve it! If it is money, we are working as hard as possible, if you get bored here, you can go back to Germany!"

My father was having financial difficulties. He came here with lots of debts from Germany. But we worked so hard to do something beneficial for the family. We would my what is we called 'meci'. We would shuck the corn, put them in a stick, and boil them in water. Then we would offer it to everyone in our village. That day I was bored a bit, so I went to take a walk. My father came next to me and said "My girl, look! Everyone is here. You should help, so that we can finish it quickly."

"Okay, but what will I get in return?"

"Like what?"

"Like school?"

"We'll see my beautiful girl, we'll see."

And it was time for enrolments.

My grandpa told my dad; "Give the ID of her, I will enrol her to the school." I do not know what they spoke before, but after that they argued. My father was shouting at my grandpa.

"I am here now, and you cannot do anything about the matters. I am her father, not you! Do not put your nose into this." I could not believe the way he talked with his father. I went a bit further toward them, because they were outside.

My grandpa told him:

"I know exactly what to do about this misconduct of yours, son! But do not worry. I am not like you, I cannot do anything to my son, but unfortunately, you are my son. You are harming this girl! May God help you." He then went to his house. I was sad and worried, because I could not understand this stiffness of my father's thought about school. My mother, on the other hand, did not care a bit, as if I am not even her child. I was telling to myself, "My mother is so cruel". After that argument, no one ever talked about this school problem. It was my father's decision. But why father changed that much? Why was he acting the way he was? Those kinds of questions were on my mind all the time, and of course, I was crying.

Sometime later, my grandpa tried to explain to me what happened. "My girl, there nothing I could do now, I'm so sorry." Aunt Mahmure was also there, and she was looking at me in jealousy, just because I am close with my grandfather. Aunt Nergiz, on the other hand, was trying to tell me something. One day she asked me "Hüsniye, why are you so close with your grandpa?", I told her "Because I'm her granddaughter?", she said "But he has lots of grandchildren". Then I asked her, "So why then aunt?", and she said:

"Well as you know, everyone calls me mixed, just because one of my parents are from Salonica, and the other on is Laz.

"So?"

"So, both of my parents are Turks. But that is not the case for you, you are mixed."

"What?"

"Yes, you are. Just think about it."

Yes, I was thinking like a mad woman. But why she told me that? I went outside, I saw my father's car. Its doors were open. I went straight into the car, and sat on the driver's seat. So, I looked inside: Steering wheel, brake, gas pedal... But then I opened glovebox. There was a notebook. Inside it, there were many notes about addresses, telephone numbers, etc... Then I found a photo. I took that photo and held it to the light to see it clearly. On that photo, my father was on a bed, with a blonde lady with short hairs. They were reading the newspaper, my father was holding one side of the newspaper, and that lady was holding the other side. I thought it was a shot from the hospital.

My father saw me in the car, and came to me. "What are you doing here?" he said. I told him "I'm just playing here," and asked him "Who's this lady?".

"I am going to give you a secret now. But it is only between us. You are not allowed to talk about that," I nodded. He made me swear, then he told me; "That lady on this shot is your mother." Just then, we saw my mother, she was going somewhere she just past front of us.

"Then who is she?"

"That woman on the photo is your birth mother, and she is the one who raised you."

I felt weird, I did not find it believable. I felt like he just told me that because he did not want me to speak about it. I did not believe him, but I felt affected. Couple of days later, I wanted to look at that book again. This time it was inside the pocket of my father's jacket. But photo was not there. I found some notes. There were a name, address, and a phone number. The writing looked like Yugoslavian to me. I checked it later; it is a writing from that is used in Georgie nowadays also. I was surprised and sad. I started to think about it. But I was not crying this time, I was just depressed. My father realised what happened, and make that book disappeared. Then he told me; "Remember the things I told you? All of them were just a joke. That woman was just a friend that just visited me". I wanted to believe my father. Because otherwise, it was too heavy to take... So, it was this feeling, being separated from your own mother. I could not come to my senses for days.

That moment, I should have tried to meet my real mother. That was the right thing to do. Kids can fell the reality, and can see what is real or not. They should be raised in the way they feel happy. But of course, within the bounds of possibility... During those year, to build a friendship with someone, you needed to give a secret, you would test them. I think that was the way it was, because I had many intimate friends.

Our beloved ones, our immediate environment, and people around us; all of them are very important for sure. We can be happy, as much as our beloved one are mature and thoughtful. Do we really know our beloved ones, are they the right people? When we try to build family bonds, we give an opportunity to other people. There might be problems within the family. About these problems, one can try to intervene with only truths, or decide to just stay away from it.

If a person takes unrelated matter personally, that basically means; that person has problems. When those kinds of people try to embarrass somebody, or take thing personal and try to prove them, they try to nit-pick others. They feel fine this way. But those people cannot be cured, because they never believe they have a problem. They always look thing in a negative way. They never feel in peace.

Unfortunately, they do not make problems just for themselves, but for the people around them either. Kids cannot choose what is right or wrong. According to the experts, a child's developments last till the age 7. During the whole seven years of our life, our character stars to get effected by those around us. If we manage to have the ability to 'self-check', then we can understand whether we have any problem, or not.

Adults around us, just say "This is right, and this is wrong", and don't care about what's left behind. How someone can feel happy, if the chain of command continues from grandfather to father and to child. What the real problem?

Is the problem just being afraid of taking responsibilities, or just trying to get an easy life? Peace is the main reason of happiness. And to find peace, you need to do the right things. The right things are what you do for your own child, even if it hurts you. This way even children comply with it. All those problems are still here today, just because we always follow the wrong path. We should try to follow the right path, with our own experiences. Instead of making things hard for people around us with anger, we should focus on ourselves, we should spend time for ourselves. How good it would be, if we can learn our children the meaning of sharing, without making a distinction between boys and girls. Our women, mothers, aunts, neighbours, girls, wives, daughters... Our circle starts with family first, then with our neighbourhood. Then it is society. All of these are our common interest, and they affect us. Negativeness kills our mood, makes us unhappy. Even though you see "Well, I don't care" about the others' problems, one should always remember that, those problems might find you in the future.

A perfect life is not possible, but we can change the way people think. If you make fun of other people's weaknesses, that means you have a problem. When we help people, we should do it with frankly. If we are not the perfect match for a problem, we should not help at all. For example, if you decide to help someone first, but then leave them alone, also affects your own mental health. You might have problems about trusting someone, but I must remind you that you are living, if you do not notice it before. You are the one who hard to trust. That because, we are not clear enough. We all should be clear. When someone asks our help, we should say yes, or no according to our possibility.

We all complain about some actions of our society. We always say things like there are no respect, or humanity anymore. But to live in a better society, first we should do better, we should be good. We do not need to spend money to give pregnant women, or old or disabled people our seat in public, it is enough to be healthy.

In order to do these kinds of civilized actions, we do not need to go developed countries. We can also feel like human, if we show our love and respect to others. First, we should understand to care about ourselves first, and then about society. We can feel, and make others feel civilized and healthy. We should be good towards other regardless of their colour or appearance. For example; rich or poor, orphan or not, alone, or not... We should remember that all of us are equal; so that we can be sure about ourselves, that we are a decent human being.

A person who undertakes factious or spoiled actions, only makes a fool of himself. Because there are different kinds of people, from different nationalities, religions, cultures. Each culture and religion have their own meanings. People follow their religions, because they believe in them. It may seem right or wrong for us, but that does not matter, it is not up for a debate. Because their beliefs are sacred for them. We can judge people by their beliefs. Faith is only between God and that person, and its judgement belongs to him/her.

Our cultural habit, are just our customs that have been going on for years. Those traditions or customs, may change from person to person, or place to place. And people may share their traditions with other. This makes people come closer. The form of celebrating something important with others has been around for years. Each society has its own traditions, and customs. This creates a diversity of cultures. And we all can be a part of this. This actions of sharing our traditions with others, and learning about other cultures, develop our general knowledge, and help us to get socialize. And of course, thanks to this, we can act justly towards other, and we can be objective towards differences.

Agony and Values

So much happened during the intervening years. Both of my uncles had a child. Uncle Abdullah began to reproach to my father, because he got married due to the imposition of my grandpa with the offer from my dad. After thing got a bit loud with my uncle and my dad, my dad talked with his friends, father of Aunt Mahmure. So, my father told him about the problems inside the house, and what made my uncle uncomfortable. Then her father had a talk with Mahmure. He told her daughter about respect. They were raised by two different families, so her father reminded her what needed to be done to made that marriage work, and then things got quiet. In the year 1980, when things were quiet, my sister got married. My mother had another girl, after an unexpected pregnancy. One of my brothers enlisted in the army to serve his service, and my younger brother was at town to study. Little later, my younger uncle went into the service of army, then he came back later. That summer was hard both for me and my older brother. We had to work so hard. Because there were no one else to help us. I and my brother did all the hard work in the field. We had no workers to help us, and there was a little baby back at our house. But I was enjoying working in the field, because things were chirpy that summer. I have always liked to work and produce things. I was so open to learn something, that why I was super happy to learn and do the thing I learned. Of course, others were aware of this characteristic of mine. So, they gave me even more work. People around started to come and said "Your girl is a woman now" to my father, because they were impressed by my hardworking nature. But my father would always tell them "Yes she is tall, and she grew up, but she's still a girl". One day some women came to us about marriage and I got angry. So, I went to my Aunt Melahat, and Aunt Nergiz to complain. They told me;

"Yes, you are not old enough to marry. But one day, you will marry someone. Why are you getting so angry about it? Do you love someone?"

"No, I am just a girl still. I still have a change to go back to the school. I am just being patient. Hopefully my father would not make a mistake and decide to marry me with someone. I do not want to marry now. I just want to go back to the school." They did not say anything.

Aunt Nergiz had her second child. It was winter. My aunt would always complain about her tonsils, and headaches. So, she wanted to go under a surgery, and she did.

But it took some time for her to came back to normal life. Two or three months later, it was time for tobacco planting. She was still complaining about her throat, she was saying there was still something wrong with her throat. We waited a bit, because we thought it would have gone back to normal. But her throat swelling was bad. She still helped us about planting, but then they went to see a doctor. Doctor told them to go to the Ankara Hacettepe University Hospital, but they went to the Samsun Medicine Faculty Hospital to get the results quickly... She went under a biopsy. Sometime later, my uncle and my aunt went to the hospital to get the results. We were really scared about it. We were trying to console ourselves by saying "She is only 21, and has two children, hopefully she'll be okay". At night, my uncle and Aunt Nergiz came back from hospital. My grandpa asked them with fear:

"What's the diagnosis?"

My aunt answered.

"Hodgkin's... It is a cancer."

My grandpa told her with a wobbly sound:

"What?"

"There's nothing to do."

And she started her treatment. She was hospitalized in Ankara Hacettepe University Hospital. We were still hopeful. She was going to be okay... And we called my aunt's father. Her father was back at Germany. They told him "Your daughter is sick. You should come here before she dies, so that she will be happy." My aunt was very keen on his father. So, his father came back to here, and they started to spend their times together. And in the meantime, my aunt's diagnosis finalized. We found out that, this disease was with her since her birth... Her tonsillectomy became the result of metastasis. Doctors told us there had been a treatment for her, and she could have been better. But my aunt even had problems while she was eating. Her treatment was harsh and expensive. But she was happy, even in that hard condition. She was also sure that she was going to die, but she was brave. She was doing her best to fight. She would always tell us "I'm fine." This alone, helped me to believe she was going to be okay. Later, she went to Ankara again, for her treatment.

The year was 1981. This time my other brother enlisted in the army. My older brother came back home from army. That summer was also hard. We dealt with all the works of field, only me and my older brother. And my father brought in a little kid to help us. His name was Murat, but I was calling him Musti, he was 7. His family was poor, and Musti was working to help them. He was just a little boy, and was working in a strange village. He felt asleep just after he came to us, he was probably too tired. But he was covered in dirt. He needed a bath. But he was just a little boy. I thought about waiting my mother, but she would have probably cared about it. So, I made the bath ready for him, I gave him clean underwear. I had never washed a kid before, but I did it. After his bath, he ate his meal, and went straight to the room we spared for him.

My brother never liked working in the field. Little Musti was helping us about grazing. But my brother was always looking for ways to make him work even more. But she was just a little boy. When my brother yelled at him, he would always come towards me to hide behind me. And I would protect him. I would fight with my brother, and I would always tell him "You need to work harder, not him!".

There was a little baby at home, so my mother was a bit busy with that. I had so many things to do both in the field, and at home. But, both of my brothers, and my mother never cared about working. And their behaviours were making things hard for me. Some of our neighbours and my friends came to helped me, and thanks to them, we managed to do thing a bit better. I was really pleased with the help I got from them. Things got a bit easy for me, but works that needed to be done had never end. There were many things to do still. It was time for mattock. During one day, little Musti was dealing with animals. He then came to me crying:

"Sister, sister! Help me!"

"What happened? Do not you worry, I'd help you."

"I was dealing with animal, but then one of the pregnant cows went straight away. I could not do anything about it, any another one started run towards the corps. I went after one of them, but then the other one went missing."

"Okay, stop crying. You had nothing to do there."

I was asking myself, why would a cow have run away. Then my father saw us, and tell me "What happened?"

"Let us make a deal first. Musti had nothing to do there. So, do not blame him. One of our cows went straight to the wilderness. So Musti went after that cow, but then another cow fled. Why did that cow run away?"

My mother agreed to me. She told me "Yes, it has nothing to do with Musti. We are not angry at him. That cow was pregnant. Maybe it was all about that. Let us start look together." Musti went to other animals to look after them. And we started looking for that cow. That was its first pregnancy, and we were worried about it. My father said "We are on our own field. We will find it; do not you worry." We looked every place. We tried our best, but could not find it. I was so worried and scared about it that I could not sleep till morning. We had two-story house, I would normally stay in the first floor, but I could not sleep in there that night because of my worries... I laid on the sofa with my daily closed, and slept there.

Then the first thing I heard was morning azan. There were voices outside, from my mum and dad. I looked outside to figure out whether there is any news. Then, the door of my room was opened. There was a shadow. That shadow told me:

"Come on, get up! Your cow gave birth. It is fine now. We took it to back of the stall. Go there. Go take it home. Come, get up!" Then the shadow disappeared. That was some kind of miracle. I got up immediately. Was that true? Or was that just my mind playing games? Did I go crazy? In order to figure it out, I needed to go there. I said 'Bismillâhirrahmânirrahîm' and went down stairs. My father and mother told me "Haven't you sleep yet?"

"Just wait a couple of minutes father, I'm coming" I said. I walked towards that stall in haste. My father was surprised. He said "What's going on?" because I would never wake up during those times. I went to the stall by passing through garden. I took almost 300 steps, then I saw it! It was there! And it was with her calf. I could not believe my eyes. And that cow got up, when it saw me. It came closer to me and smelled me. That was her first calf. It was like; it was trying to tell me "I'm good with my calf." And I started crying, but I was happy! They were happy tears. It had such a good calf... I took the calf with me, and three of us started walking towards our house. My father had followed me. So, he saw me with the cow and its calf. He was shocked. When he saw us, he started praying. He said "We searched it for hours!". I told my father what happened.

"I could believe it but a shadow was in my room and told me this place."

My father was still praying. But I was happy, because I filled with peace. That was a great end... That thing got me thinking. Yes, animals were not be able to talk with us, but they were expressing their feeling still. What was the difference between us then? It was only our appearance, and we were speaking, that is it...

After that experience, I started questioning whether I should eat meat or not. Was that necessary to eat meat, after such an experience? It was not a problem according to our religion, but I was still feeling bad about it.

By the way, my aunt came back to us, but she was very slim now. I asked my uncle:

"Uncle, she got treated, but why did she get so slim?

"Yes, she got her treatment, but her treatment made his body weak. That is why she lost so much weight. But now her treatment is done. Hopefully she will get better."

"So, doctors told you she'll get better?"

"Yes, they did."

In the meantime, one of my grandpa's brothers were also undergoing a treatment for cancer, but we lost him. Everyone went his funeral, so I was responsible from the house that day. And they did not tell anything about the funeral to my aunt, because they did not want her to lose hope. My aunt was lying on her bed, it had been just a couple of days. I was watching her by a distance not to cause any disturbance. That day I went straight to her room. I wanted to see her. She was sleeping, but she woke up. Then called me. "Come here girl, I need to talk to you."

"Sure aunt."

"I know that man has died due to cancer. So, do not try to hide things from me."

"Yes, aunt. Everyone went his funeral, but I am here for you."

"Thank you. I want to tell you about life."

"Okay aunt, I'm listening."

"My girl, I will die soon. I know that. I am not going to get treated. I know you are looking at me that way. I do not want to make you sad, but I also trust you. You are such a good person, and you are smart too. Look here, do not make yourself sad just because they did not let you go to the school. I am sure you will do something nice for yourself after I die. He will take my little son İskender from your older uncle. He will take care of him just like his sons. He is only one year old. That is why I am sure my God, and they will take care of him. Then my older son; Veli. I am sure he will be looked after well; he will get his education. But in a short span of time, you will go somewhere distant, and Veli will also go there just a little later. You need to take care of him. You should be his sister. You should see him as your own brother. Even he did bad, or say something bad, please look after him. You will get sad about me first, but you will find peace."

I was just listening her there in complete surprised feelings. I told her:

"Your children are already my brothers. Of course, I will take care of them." But I was feeling weird.

"You will be better. I heard what they said."

"Do not believe them. They are just lying." And the conversation ended just like that. My aunt was very sick, so it was hard for her to speak so long.

After that talk with my aunt, I was even more mature now. I started thinking about what we talked. I was just a kid. Where would I go even? Or that thing about my real mother is true? Will my father send me to my real mother?

My aunt was under pain killers special for her, but her condition was getting worse. It had been one month since the death of that uncle. Grandpa Leman came us about the death of my uncle from Trabzon. It was Friday. Everyone went to the Friday prayers. Grandpa told his 'get well soon wishes' to my aunt. My uncle would stay awake at night to look after his wife. When my father got there, he had fallen asleep. My grandpa performed ablution and started praying. My aunt passed away even before my grandpa finished his prayers. May God rest her soul… Then, they woke up my uncle. My uncle tried to close his death wife's eyes, but could not do it. Because she left her children, and beloved ones behind. She had two children, one of them was three, and the other one was only one. She had always loved girl, and she had been praying to have baby girl.

We all were filled with sadness. The things my aunt told me was still around my mind. My aunt's mother, and other relatives buried her in her funeral. By the nature of our traditions, women would not go to the cemeteries during funerals. Us, the women, would go back to the house. Many of them were still crying around the house. Men stayed in the cemetery for a long time. They prayed. Then they came back. My aunt's older son came towards me.

"Sister! We are here."

There were bunch of daisies on his hand. He passed them to me.

"Sister, my uncles buried my mother. So, I put many flowers on her grave." He was looking inside my eyes.

"You did good" I said. I was going to hug him, but he started crying, and running.

"My mother will not be with me anymore!"

I was going to go with him, but one of our older neighbours hold me.

"Let him cry. He should cry, you should cry. It is better to cry, in order to accept the reality of it.", was that really the right thing not to go with him? But she was the older one, so I stayed there. But if I had turned back in time, I would have gone with him. He was with his peers.

Life must go on, and so it did. My older uncle's wife Melahat had never kids. So, she took Veli and İskender with joy. She looked after them carefully. And my step-grandma, my grandpa's second wife, also helped her. Kids were loved by everyone, and they were in good hands. We all prayed for her, and did everything we could, but now it was time for the goodbye.

Lie and Accusation

The year was 1982. Even though there were many things to get sad, we also had to fight for our future, for the future we do not know yet, because we were a family. My father was a bit softer towards me now, because he also was familiar with my strong characteristics. I had gone a course to be a tailor before, but I have never liked dealing with dresses. That year we also planted the fruits and vegetables that we can plant in winter, so we had an extra income. This way, we were getting closer to my father's dream. He wanted open a place on his field. We were getting closer with my father. I told my father;

"Dad, I am old enough now. If you allow me, I would like to work as a hairdresser and study in the same time," my father said "Okay my girl". And as a result of that, I was happy. But that winter, we could not figure out where to stay, so I could not initiate my plan.

Terrorist actions were halted after the year 1980. Things were safer. And my father was being nicer to me. He was taking me whatever I wanted, he was having conversations with me, and he was making suggestions about my plans.

I would always listen news on radio. It was passed on me by my grandpa. I heard that the prime minister enacted a law about farmers: from then on, farmers could also get retired by paying its price. That was a great news. Because farmers would always work hard, but when they would turn old, they would have nothing on their hands to live a peaceful life. Health insurance was such a great thing for farmers. I told about it to my father immediately. I told him all the necessary steps, and he also liked this idea. So, he started making his payments.

With the help of my brothers, we started the construction of our place. The first floor had already been done. My older brother went to İstanbul, because he had never fonded field works, and started working there. My other brother was more a hard worker person than my older brother. He would always help me with my works, and we would always work in cooperation. We were having a talk with my mother about the thing we had done.

I said "Your dreams will come true; we will have a beautiful house in Bafra soon". But she was looking at me scary, like I did something wrong... Her actions had never been rational. I would not get answer to my questions ever. She said "Yes, we are rich. All these field are ours, and we have our place back at city too." And I wanted to make her happy more, and said "Yes, hopefully I would also go to school." But then with anger she said "You will never turn back to the school. It is over now." I told her, "It is never over. I will turn back."

"You are telling me I am your mother, but you are never supporting me. What is wrong with you?"

"You can go back" she said. Apparently, my older brother Mesud was the one who picked for school, and I would help him with his homework.

"You are sending him, but he does not even want it. But I want it so bad, and you do not want me to go there."

"Because I'm his mother."

"And not mine?"

"Yours too."

"I am not sure about that. But I cannot help him with his homework. I do not even know the subject he's studying."

The way she talked, and her actions were killing me. But what could I have done? My mother had mental problems. She was trying to pull the subject to the traditions.

Just like every year before, we started working in summer. Everyone was on fields, and gardens... But summer was fun. Then sister of my aunt's husband came to Türkiye from abroad. And my aunt also came here with her to my grandpa's. My grandpa's house and ours was right next to each other. So, I would always see who passed there. That lady started to talk with everyone. Apparently, she was looking for a candidate for his son. I complained about her. What was she thinking? She was trying to pick a girl, just like picking a fruit in a shop. How disrespectful was that?

Most would not like her. My brother Mesud once had fun with her son. He said to me "He was eating like he came from Africa but not Australia". And I told him "Yes, you are right. And he even does not like us. What a prick".

In the end, we were all relatives. That was why no one was telling anything. One day, someone told my father about me, and he said that person; "My girl is still just a little girl. Tell her to find herself a bride somewhere else!".

We were dealing with field works, but people were coming and going to our house... There was something going on. Apparently, that whole thing was not over yet. Some people tried to make that desire real, so Pakize came to our house to marry me to her son. My older uncle's wife Melahat told me "We did not ask you. But we agreed to marry you with her son. What do you say?" and I told her "You are saying 'you agreed', and now asking my thoughts?". I did not know what to say. I was surprised.

Things I said was not listened correctly. But my father told them to go away, how did he change his mind? What was going on? What was the rush?

My mother was looking at me in anger.

"What are you looking at me like that? Why did my father change his mind?"

"I don't care and I don't know."

Then we went to shopping, we visited the family. That visit was about the wedding. The woman was telling us that she would take everything from Australia, and she would make two wedding just for his son. She was making us look like idiots.

When we came back to our house, I told my family I had not wanted to marry him. My mother did not even listen. She had some problem about hearing, but whenever something that she did not want to hear happened, she would not hear it. When I told other about it, no one did not even care about it. It was like talking with walls.

It was a tradition, before you go out for your wedding, you would kiss your mother's and father's hands. But my mom did not let me do it, and in fact, she shooed me away. She said "Just go now, I don't want to see you." I was embarrassed and angry. I was asking myself "What did I do wrong?"

In the wedding night, Pakize did not care for anyone. I told my uncle and my aunt "Please, let go back together. I do not love him anyway." But they said "It is the wedding night, it would not. be right to do that."

After three days later from wedding, my brother invited us, and a week later we went there to visit. There were many people there. But my father did not even get up to greet us. He was angry. My mom came to me and said "Your father wants you back, he changed his mind." Apparently, they told my father that I said "I love him, if you don't let me marry him, I will flee." It was a huge lie! A marriage arranged with lies...

I was still a girl, but even I was good enough to understand things were not okay... But even once I could not express myself. Why all these things were happening? They told me my father had changed his mind, but it was a nonsense. Was that the value of my life? I was being played like a toy.

I refused my father's request. I asked my mother about it.

"I told you that I did not want to marry, I told that to you, my mother. But you told me that was final, my father would not have changed his mind. So, I got married, and now you told me you had wanted me back!"

"That how your father is."

There was a huge argument. Both families were great at making things miserable. No one were educated enough to think about others.

After the procedures of families, now it was time for official procedures. I had been told that, in order to go to Germany, my father changed my birth date. So, I was still too young to marry. We submitted a petition to the court to fix it. In the meantime, we found out that there was an official complaint about my father. I was scared to hear that. What could have my father done?

My father, my mother and I were called by court. We went there, it was Samsun Civil Court.

"Now my girl, it is about your father. If they asked about your age, tell them you are 16. You are not married, but engaged. Your mother is Makbule, and your father is Mikail. That is, it."

They told me to remember all of them. Some people told us what to do, in order to save my father from a possible fine. Frankly, I, too, did not want my father to get fined. Anyway, we went inside a room. A document was opened, and the judge read it.

There was a woman called Margred. I did not even remember her last name now. She submitted an official complaint about a possible detainment of her child, which is 14-year-old, and a forced marriage.

It was like there were hammers inside my mind, putting a nail in every sentence. I was shocked completely. I turned away and looked at my father. He was all red. That made me even worry more.

They started to take our statements. My mother and father told the judge that they did not know that lady, there were not no children like mentioned, and it might have been a result of a hostility. It was my time. The judge asked me "Who's your mother?" I told him "My mother's Makbule", then he said "Who's your father?", I said "Mikail", and it was over. The case was closed.

Just like they told me, I saved my father. But I realised what happened. No one were telling me the truth. Everyone trying to avoid me. "We don't know that lady, and we don't know why she did such a thing" they were saying to me. Then why she was trying to do such a thing? That lady was a mother, who was trying to save her own child, and I was that child in fire. But things were going according to the plans of those who hate me. I felt like time was on their side. I was being used.

My life went sideways. I was at the beginning of the road yet. I was stressed about that. I was asking questions about this all the time. But my mother was telling me "How do you say such things my girl? You are my girl. I do not know that woman. Yes, she had a child, but her child died". Then I looked at my father. My father nodded. I was feeling too weird to do anything, but I was sure that my father would not have told me any lies. That was the important thing here. He would not do such a thing to me. No, it could not be.

In the meantime, I was talking with my relatives, with my aunt to make this easy for me, and understand them. But my father was an angry man, and my mother was weird. She was just a bad mother; I was sure that she was going to do anything to put me out of that home...

My mother-in-law Pakize went abroad. One day, I went to my grandpa's and asked him who lied about my intentions on marriage. I told him "Dad, I must recognize my enemies." He just told me a name: "Mahmure." He was also feeling sad about me, but he wanted me to go to my husband. He was thinking that, staying away from there would have helped me.

In the year 1980, there was a military coup in Türkiye. That is why, all the cases on courts were going very slowly. They were being checked even more now, and regularly. In the meantime, I lived with my ex-husband, grandmother, and uncle for 2 years. During those 2 years, I had witnessed many weird stuffs. Things had started bad, but they were being nice to me. Grandmother had some traditions. Their ways of living were different considering my own family. I was trying to understand her. By the way, I was trying to talk with my mother.

They told me to remember all of them. Some people told us what to do, to save my father from a possible fine. Frankly, I, too, did not want my father to get fined. Anyway, we went inside a room. A document was opened, and the judge read it.

There was a woman called Margaret. I did not even remember her last name now. She submitted an official complaint about a possible detainment of her child, which is 14 years old, and forced marriage.

It was like there were hammers inside my mind, putting a nail in every sentence. I was shocked completely. I turned away and looked at my father. He was all red. That made me even worry more.

They started to take our statements. My mother and father told the judge that they did not know that lady, there were not any children like mentioned, and it might have been a result of hostility. It was my time. The judge asked me "Who's your mother?" I told him "My mother's Makbule", then he said "Who's your father?", I said "Mikhail", and it was over. The case was closed.

Just like they told me, I saved my father. But I realized what happened. No one was telling me the truth. Everyone trying to avoid me. "We don't know that lady, and we don't know why she did such a thing" they were saying to me. Then why she was trying to do such a thing? That lady was a mother, who was trying to save her child, and I was that child in fire. But things were going according to the plans of those who hate me. I felt like time was on their side. I was being used.

MY DESTINY AGAINST THEIR LIES WHERE IS MY MOTHER?

My life went sideways. I was at the beginning of the road yet. I was stressed about that. I was asking questions about this all the time. But my mother was telling me "How do you say such things my girl? You are my girl. I do not know that woman. Yes, she had a child, but her child died". Then I looked at my father. My father nodded. I was feeling too weird to do anything, but I was sure that my father would not have told me any lies. That was the important thing here. He would not do such a thing to me. No, it could not be.

In the meantime, I was talking with my relatives, with my aunt to make this easy for me and understand them. But my father was an angry man, and my mother was weird. She was just a bad mother; I was sure that she was going to do anything to put me out of that home...

My mother-in law Pakize went abroad. One day, I went to my grandpa's and asked him who lied about my intentions on marriage. I told him "Dad, I must recognize my enemies". He just told me a name: "Mahmure." He was also feeling sad about me, but he wanted me to go to my husband. He was thinking that staying away from there would have helped me.

In the year 1980, there was a military coup in Türkiye. That is why, all the cases in courts were going very slowly. They were being checked even more now, and regularly. In the meantime, I lived with my ex-husband grandmother and uncle for 2 years. During those 2 years, I witnessed many weird kinds of stuff. Things had started bad, but they were being nice to me. Grandmother had some traditions. Their ways of living were different considering my own family. I was trying to understand her. By the way, I was trying to talk about my mother. Her grandson, my ex-husband, went to abroad almost a month later of his mother.

There were many rules of old grandmother. Clean the house, floor, windows, do not wait like that, always do something... I would always say "God, give me patience!" I would go to my uncle's whenever I got bored. At my uncle's I was talking about what was going on, and then my aunt said:

"Well, you will live, what you did eventually. They were also annoyed me much. His bitch told everything about me to my father. But I know what to do that bitch..." I was bewildered to hear all of these.

"Who are you talking about? If you are talking about my father, just remember that you are married just because of him, he helped you! And who is that bitch? My mom, me, my sister?"

She said "I know her well, and she knows me don't you worry." Then I told her "Well, tell me too! So that I know what is going on."

The process of my case at court about my age took half and a year. In the meantime, I was fined by old grandmother, and my fine was only eating to help my survive. She was taking of her revenge about her past on me. She felt powerful that way.

After things got cleared at court, I got my new identity card with my new birth date. And that husband of me, applied for me. There was an out for, at least it seemed like that. I went to my fathers to tell what happened. But I told my mother what I spoke with Mahmure. My mother laughed.

"You are in-low's wife is calling you bitch, and you are smiling?! That means you are not my real mother. Can you tell me the name of that bitch, my real mother?"

"No, I'm your mother," she was stuttering.

"So, you're that bitch?"

We were at kitchen. My mother left there, then my father came to me with a good laugh. But then he was shaking his head in anger. Just couple of minutes later, my mother came back to the kitchen.

"Mahmure acts wrong. She was not even thinking, when speaking. She is inconsiderate, and irrational."

For me, everyone was irrational. But I did not know what to do. Who was right? People, I thought were right, were doing terrible things, and vice versa. But how would I find the reality? There were many questions inside my mind again...

It was time to go abroad, to my husband. But people around me were not mature, or pragmatic, contrary they were mean and rude. That was even the case for my own family. For them, brides are treated almost as slaves. They have no rights; they need to accept whatever told to them. Happiness was just a dream under these conditions. Marriage has always seen as something serious here. It has been told "You need to be clever and patient, you leave your home in a wedding dress, and you turn back in graveclothes." For people, marriage should be done only once and need to last till the end. They have been told this way for a long time. And it really is like that, people usually do not want to leave their own family, the family they created from scratch, because for them, that family is the real home. The family, you did your best to make it something real, is just the people you spent the best years of your life. How painful it is that, people are not capable enough to see their brides as their daughters, and they do not protect them just like one. Contrary, they act like brides are foes or rivals, and turn the home they share into a bedlam. When you look from this page, it seems like it is nearly impossible to live a happy life, but we will live through it.

During those year, it was believed that getting divorce was not allowed by our religion. And things were on my mind again. I asked my grandpa:

"Grandpa, I know marriage is a sacred bond. And I know it is good deed to do everything possible to protect your family, raise your children. But in contrast? You are doing your best, but your partner does not even care about it. He does not treat you, or your children right. So, do I have to live with that kind of man, till I die? Is that what our religion says?"

"No, my dear girl. It is just a custom in our society. Getting married is a religious duty, but getting divorced is also allowed. You can get divorced if one of the partners is not doing things accordingly. But you should always be patient. It is easy to get things going with a nice people, but the real challenge is the contrary. You should get away from the damaging problems. You fight for yourself, hopefully Allah helps you."

We went to my ex-mother-in-law to welcome her with my aunt Mahmure and my uncle. Little later, I received an invitation letter from Ankara about my application. Many were happy for me. We went to Ankara with my ex-mother-in-law, the road trip was verry fun. We went to visit their relatives. They were looking at me, only smiling. I felt like they loved me. We went to the consulate for interview. It went fine, I felt like everything was going to be okay.

During those times, I had another experience about magic. A person came to us, he was staying with us. Others were trying to convince him about marriage. He said "If I like her, then we can do this," but he did not like what he saw. Then, they made a meal, they mixed almost everything and made him ate it. Next morning, he was saying, he was in love with that girl, and wanted to marry with her. People around us were saying "Wow, look at that. Hodja really did his job."

Those things were real. I do not think they can be coincidence.

My ex-mother-in-law started to treat me differently. Her 'nice human' mode was over. They were speaking about that magical meal, and I got worried about myself. I asked others; "I am worried about myself. Should I go to a hodja? Maybe someone did something to me."

My uncle and my aunt were tenants. One day, I went there and run into their landlord. I said "Hey, I got some worries. Weird things have been going on. I want to go and see a hodja. I want to know whether someone made a spell on me or not. Do you know anyone?"

She said: "Well, I sent your uncle's wife someone two-three weeks before. You can learn his name from your aunt."

"Thank you" I said. When we just finished our talk with landlord, my aunt opened their apartment's door. She saw us and her face turned red. That lady told me "Well ask your aunt now, she'll send you there." I went inside.

"What are you going to tell me with?"

"That lady said she had sent you to a hodja. I got some worries to. Will you take me him?"

"What's that?" She was overreacting. "I do not know what you are talking about. I cannot take you there."

She was always like that, so I did not care. Her normal was like that. This case was closed just like that. Then I got my ticket to Australia. It was time to get ready to go there. I needed to go each one of my relative before I went. We were sending letter to each other with my ex-husband, but it was over for a little while. Later I found out that, my mother-in-law did not even post them to my husband. She was always telling bad things about me. I did not totally understand what happened, but her neighbours kick her out of their homes, and never talked with her again. She was still talking with other neighbours. But then, they did the same thing, they stopped talking with her. Because all of them were good people, who understood me and my pain.

Even my neighbours were being nice to me, but when it comes to my relatives, it was like talking to a wall. Only my father was reacting things. My ex-mother-in-law told me, if I could not receive the visa to go Australia, she would marry her son with someone else. I told her that this was a matter of honour, and if she did such a thing, I would do the necessary thing very quickly. I also told her that I got my father's word.

You cannot make fun about everything in this life. If you hurt other people's honour and morals, a bit later you will taste your own medicine. These kinds of people would never be brave enough to talk to your face, they would always do things behind your back, they lie easily.

Before we went to Australia, I had wanted to go back to my brothers and sister to spend some time with them. They said OKAY. So, I went back to my village, to say goodbye to my beloved ones, and I did say goodbye. I was going with a problematic marriage to a strange land, from my own homeland... In such problems, people would normally abandon their own family and their own country. I did not have such a feeling, but I was not completely sure about it. I was getting ready with the feeling of everything could get fine when we get face to face with my husband. I was really affected; my senses were mixed all over my mind. My tears did not stop even once for three or four days.

I went to İstanbul, after I said goodbye to everyone in Samsun, Bafra and our village. My brother got me from the terminal. My brother was staying with his friends, I went to my sister's place. I told my brother:

"Bro, I had problems about marriage, and I was thinking about getting here, to you. I would look for a job, and study."

"You would not stay with me, but we would take care of it. Hopefully you will be happy now."

My brother and I did some visits to our relatives there. He paid all necessary things. He did all the plans. I was unfamiliar with these good deeds of my brother. My brother was a better person, at least I felt like that. İstanbul did some good work on him... I was happy about it. My sister had had her second child, and they were all good. They all had a proper life there, so I was going to leave there with a happy face.

It was time to leave İstanbul behind. I went to a hairdresser with my last money. They did me a weird bun hair, but I liked it. We went to the airport with my brother. My ex-mother-in-law and her friend had already been there. With me, there was another new bride. We all met there to travel. We had a little talk with all of them, and I met with two other women. Then we hugged with my brother. My brother told me to take care myself:

"Write to us all the time. Write to each one of us every week, and take care yourself."

It was a touching moment… It was the most touching moment I had for a while. That one week with my brother and my sister was good for me. It was my first in there, in İstanbul. Now it was my first time to fly. And our journey began. All the things happening in the plane were all new to me… It took full two days to get there. İstanbul – Belgrade – Melbourne and Sydney. We went there with Yugoslavian Air. It was horribly far away; it could not end soon enough. Most of their beloved ones were on the airport to meet with them… My husband was also there, but he was cold towards me. Even some of their neighbours came to meet with us. It was the year 1984, and October. There were very less people from Turkey there, so they would always go to airport to meet and greet them, so that they would not feel alone. They were telling things like: "Look, you came here from that far away, but we are here as Turks." It was a great behaviour of them. Our Turkish neighbours was still coming to our home. No one had that weirdness of my mother-in-law. She was all over us of me and my husband, she would have even tried to split our beds, if she had the power to do it. She was doing her best to not let things go easy. I was the main topic almost every day of her talks. She would always say something bad about me every day. I, on the other hand, was just trying to follow things around. When she was saying things about me, I was just telling "What, me? No" kinds of things. That was a result of the customs: older people are always right. But when I was being nice, and doing all the errands in the house, she was telling me bad things, she talking bad about my honour, she was telling how messy I was, how bad I was. And I needed to share the same house with that woman, because I was married...

I was a stranger in Sydney. I did not know English. Even other Turks there was speaking English, and I did not even know anyone. My only job was to stay at home, cook meal for other, clean the house, and do the other chores. My mother-in-law, on the other hand, was always talking with other, gossiping around, and talking on phone, because otherwise she got bored. She started to hide the meals in the house. She would take our meal to the neighbours. She would always go outside, and there would be nothing to eat at house. The guy I married was working, and I did not even know where he was working. Later I found out that he was working in a McDonald's, and my mother-in-law would go to her son to eat there. I asked my husband:

"So said you were studying electrical engineering?"

His answer was already ready.

"Schools are not open yet, so I'm working to make a bit more earning."

"Yes, sure. Good."

Of course, he was lying. Later, he studied at a private school to be a technician. So, he never went to a university. Anyway, at least he tried his best. But I was got lied on my face, and it was not just a simple thing. If you lie someone, you take the chance of being happy.

One day our neighbour Belkıs came at us.

"Can I check your fridge if I may?"

"Yes, but there's nothing inside it, why do you want to check it?"

She said, "But this fridge is working?"

I said "Yes." She told me that my mother-in-law put all the foods in house to Belkıs' fridge, because she told her that our fridge had broken. It was hard to believe; she was even trying to hide foods from me. Later, Belkıs sent all the foods to our house. So, finally I had some food to cook some meal. I would always cook the meal, and set the table, but she would come and send me somewhere. When I came back, there would be no food to eat, and she would tell me "Oops, it's all gone." I was being treated at that house even worse than an animal. They were all weird, they were trying to be happy over your sadness. Later, Belkıs started to take me whenever she went to the city centre. She would tell "I am going to the centre. She should come with me; she would be a friend". Or she would take me to their home. So that, I would eat some proper food this way. By the way, we were having financial problems. So, they sent me to social security network to get money from there. I was there as a fiancée of a man, this way either I would be get taken care of by someone else, or I should marry with my husband. So, this way, official procedures about our marriage had started…

I started an English course to learn how to speak it. I was living under the watch of government and was taking education. The money from social securities was coming via mail. I was not even aware that I was getting money back then. My father-in-law would take that money. You will get treated as the way you treat others. People's feelings are reflected on their actions.

Belkıs was taking me with herself even more now. Our family doctor was Indonesian, and he was Muslim. He would come to our house sometimes. When he came, he would always analyse what was going around. With his analysis, even he understood me. One day, I told Belkıs that I was feeling weird. There was a problem with my stomach, and I had not been menstruated for days. So, we went to doctor. He drew my blood to make the necessary analysis. Then we went to city centre with Belkıs. We were on the line of a bank, and suddenly I fainted. Belkıs was speaking with the teller, and I told her "I can't see." She was still speaking, and I told her the same thing. I tried my best to open my eyes, but then felt down. Everyone got flurried at bank. When I opened my eyes, I was at hospital. I asked "What happened to me?" they said "Don't worry, there's nothing wrong, we'll tell you what happened."

A little later, I was told that I was pregnant. Belkıs congratulate me and said "The baby's coming!" I told her "Wow, am I really pregnant?"

"Yes, this baby will bring peace to you. Everyone back at home will be happy to hear this. In the end, this will be their first grandson!" I was watching her, while she was telling me those things. I was wondering whether it was true? People back at home would really feel happy? We would have seen their reactions, when we get there...

That day was wild. I was fainted first, and I learned that I was pregnant. We were late. We went to our house in a haste. Belkıs told everyone "Yes, we are late. But we are great news. You are going to have a grandson!". My mother-in-law was not happy to hear it, as if she was almost going to have a heart attack. Then there was almost a war in that house. She was telling me how could've this happened... She was all around us, me, and my husband, but was still in shock. I told Belkis that "you said she was going to be happy. She has no limit; she is a maniac". And she told me "Well, you are really right about that."

That day passed away like that. Her talks with other, phone calls were never ending. They lasted for days. Then I found out what was going on. She was still angry; she was screaming in the middle of our living room.

"She is just a headache to us! She is carrying her father's bastard. That bastard is not from my son!" She was screaming like mad! She started to run towards me. She was cursing me also. She would always insult me in our Turkish neighbourhood, she would always insult me. In order to humiliate me even more, she called the mosque. She told them that I was dirty, my baby was not from my husband, but from my lover. That exact moment, I felt my mother instincts. I was extremely angry, and I did not just stay quiet that time. I hold her hairs and told her; "If you have the courage to tell the truth, you would tell your dirty secrets!"

We fought from tooth to nail. I even forgot that I was pregnant. I was in shock, and I was not someone with experience. We fought for a while. I warned her by saying "If you ever say anything to accuse both me and my baby, I'll rip your devil tongue off your mouth." I grabbed her tongue. Her screams were so loud that, it probably was heard from afar. Some came inside after hearing the screams. I was crying for the things she had done to me before, all the tortures and accusations. I lost my control and beat her so bad. But the ones who came to intervene criticized me as if they never heard her words before. I stamped as the bride who beat her mother-in-law. They told me, I had fancied myself as something, and I should have been handed to the police…

"Oh no! Look at that! The bride's beating her mother-in-law!"

"Till the day I came here, you are treating me like a dog. I came here from Türkiye, but where do you think you come from? One should always remember her roots. And should not do the things she does not want to experience. But you are just watching, and having fun with all the problems I have been experiencing, like you have nothing else to do. I am from a very decent family; I have been raised as a decent person. I have been raised so decent that, I stayed silence to all your bad talks. You left me with no food in this house, but I made you meals every day! I made tea for you. But here you are, putting all the blame on me, like you have never seen what she has been doing to me! I understand that, my family was decent. Because at this age, I am a better person than all of you! I can see your personalities now, very clearly! Yes, I beat my mother-in-law. It is right or wrong, but I have no regrets. You are calling me impudent, but I can also beat you, remember! So, it is better for you to go to your homes!"

At the same time, Belkıs said about me:

"What she did was just a self-defence. You can call the police, if you want. But there something you all forget. You pushed her hard till this day. There is a huge provocation against her. So, of course, police will ask about the reason behind this fight, and so, she will tell what was happening. And, she is pregnant! It is a lawless act to try beat a pregnant woman. Here, the government, cares much about pregnant women, and their babies. But if you still want to call them, you should. So that you can lock yourselves up."

I went to my room. I was still angry, and it took a good time to get calm. My god! I was inside the hell, what did I do to deserve all these things? I took a rest at my room. Then, I went out of my room. Things were quiet, and no one was talking. There were many foods at kitchen. Surprising… Then I remembered a saying: Spare the rod, and spoil the child. So, I thought it was true. They got decent in the end, but it took some beating to make them. How weird…

After couple of days, Belkıs came over and told me what happened. They even tried to lock me up by going to doctors to get a report. They went to our family doctor. Then, Indonesian doctor Peter told my father-in-law: "Yes, you have bruises. But I did not see what happened. So, I cannot give you a report. You are telling it was your bride. If you behave nicely, I do not think anything like this happen in the future."

They did everything to get that report, but he rejected all. That man was protecting me, even though he was a family, or a fellow citizen. He was just a decent person, who managed to see what is right and wrong. Whenever I would visit him, he would do everything to make me save something. He was like a father to me. He once told me: "I also have kids. I would not want them to experience such things. You should really get familiar with the man you will get married." God bless his soul; he died couple of years ago.

Mother-in-law and her son went to Türkiye, after that incident. Her son went to enlist the army, and she went there to have a vacation. Well, of course, it was long. I was all alone during my pregnancy. I met with a man; whose name was Bekir. He was trying to help me about my brother, because I wanted him to get here. He was an employee in an association. He initiated the process. But there was no positive reply to the application. I had no one there, besides my neighbours. I continued my English course for a while. But I was in peace. No more fights, only peace.

I gave birth to a baby girl in the year 1985, and I was all alone again. During the birth, Belkıs' sister Ferda was with me. But my fears were still there. I feared the things I should not have scared. Besides the family I am sharing that home with, everything there was great: Laws, women rights, opportunities, and even people. But I was not aware all these things. Because I had no time to think about them in details. There was only one detail that I was obsessed with: Why those things are always happening to me? Why all those people are negative towards me? There was no moral support from the man I married, or from his family, or from even my family. But I was unaware of my family. There were throwing me into the fire in my single mistake.

I was in a hole again, and I was unable to fill that hole. I was trying to get the bottom of the problem. When I was pregnant, I was all aware that they were only going to accept my baby, if it is a boy. That was a disgusting feeling. It was my baby in the end! What an impudence

that was! They were even having fights with about my unborn child… I complained about my husband to the consulate. They told him it was required from him to accept that children, otherwise it would bring a sentence to him, at least 9 months. This was submitted to his address in Türkiye.

In our marriage, there were hurt feelings, there were no love, respect, or trust. I did not need to face that problem that long. But reactions from my family were keep coming. Problems, and accusations were still there. My baby, on the other hand, was just a little human being. We started working with Belkıs' mother at home. We were knitting for clothing stores. I tried my best to earn just a bit enough to buy baby food for my child.

The day my daughter turned one, I wanted to have a job. And so, I did. I was working in a sheet factory, and I was responsible for packaging. Owners of that factory were from Cyprus. And I realised the importance of money at that job. We still had a long way to go, and I needed to find a nanny for my daughter. We started working somehow. There were also my neighbours there, we created a working team. On my side, things started to go to the good side. And one day, that man I was married with, was back. We decided to give a try to our marriage just because our child, so we moved in with him to another house. I gave all my savings to my father-in-law, with the feeling of 'everything will be fine when we get our new house.' But of course, things did not go as planned. I was being discriminated on the money I saved. They started to take my money. I was trying to fight with them to get something new to my house. So, there were nothing changed. It was just a dream to have a proper life, with love, respect, and trust, with this family. So, that marriage was over first in my mind, then in my hearth. Either I have a normal marriage just like normal people, or it is better to end things… You should try to do the right thing, not just for yourself, but for your daughter also. But my daughter was also lacking all the love and respect from this family, just because she was my daughter. There was no future for us, either I would have lived there like a captive, or I would have gone elsewhere. I was demanding a normal life for my daughter. But I was not stupid enough to support people's life by working so hard. Either I had the love and respect I deserved, or things would have gone sideways. In such break ups, people tend to forget justice, and faith. You need justice to be equal with everyone, and for your own child. At least, I should have gotten what they took from me. Because I was going to be all alone after that, and so it happened. My daughter was closer to me than my loneliness. But her father was going away, by alleging excuses. Just because I tried and worked hard to earn for my life and my daughter's life... I was just a normal thing to do. Everyone can work, and decide to take steps for their own lives. Why am I worthless? And if I am worthless, why do they take what I have? It was not about faith, or race. It was just an act of impudence, and that thing was not only making me angry, but also was making me sick. I do not want a single penny from an undeserved money, and I do not want to live an undeserved life, good or bad. You can only spend a poor life with people with poor morals... But a decent life, can only be achieved with the decent people, and by doing the right thing. I wanted a decent life with love and respect. And I wanted it to happen just with my daughter, even if she would be far away from me. I was time to end the things that had made me peaceless. So, I told my husband, who was going away just to 'give me a lesson': "You are the one that needs a lesson, not me. I do not want in my life anymore. You can only do a last favour both me and your daughter. Give back the money you took from me." But of course, my offer was rejected. Courts, and courts again... The case was still on the court, but father-in-law sent me a message:

"My wife made you to break up. I am sad about this. You should come to have a talk, please."

I told him: "I cannot trust you anymore. Because I will not trust people who lies all the time."

"What I can do to earn your trust?" he said.

"You are a faithful person. If you performed an ablution and swear on Quran, I can believe you."

He told me "Yes, not a problem, just come here." So, I went there, he performed his ablution.

"She is, my granddaughter. I do not want her to suffer. As you can see, I did whatever you told me. Now I am putting my hand on Quran. I swear, I do not want you guys to break up."

I was really surprised to see this. If I had rejected him, then I would have been the one with bad intentions. He swore to help me, but I would have been the one who decided to break up, if I rejected to reunite with my husband. I said "Let's try one last time", so we were reunited.

They got the news about my grandpa's condition. They told me "You should go there, and see him." I was anxious, but I was also dying to see my family. I had been six years. They were getting everything, but I was the one who was working. Anyway, I took my chances. And I continue that.

The date was January 16th, 1991. It was the first visit to my family, to my homeland since the day I left. When I got there, I went straight to my grandpa. My grandpa would always greet me in the living room. But I did not see him there. Then they told me he died, but I did not want to believe that. I heard so many lies that, I wanted to see him with my own eyes. So, I did see with my own eyes, and my grandpa had really died… I feel into pieces. He was the closest person to me in this family. I am sure that he would have told me what to do in my life, but I was away.

I stayed there for 6 months. I bought a field with the money I saved. I, and my father, and my mother, visited all our relatives.

Wherever we went, people would tell me: "I got sick because of her. She is always anxious, so we also feel anxious. We do not care if she is here or not, the only thing we care is to hear that she is doing well." During the holiday period, I did not visit my husband's family. But my mother sent me there, and fought with me to make me do it. I went there, but I wanted to stay away from there, because I was the one to blame there. Old grandma there told me: "I really missed you. I am happy you are here. I had made a lemonade, but I did not drink it yet. You should drink."

I took a sip from that lemonade, but there was a smell of soap in it. They were all clean people, but there was an intense smell of soap. So, I pour it to the sink, and I told her: "I'm sorry, but it smells like soap, I can't drink it." I stayed there, in Samsun, for couple of days. But I was not fond of them. I was there just because my mother made me do it.

People were criticizing me, just because I bought a piece of land by myself. They were saying: "You should be ashamed. A woman should not get a land on by her own when she is married." I was telling them: "I don't respect the person I don't trust." I was away from him. Yes, one should share what she has with her husband, if he also helps, but that is not the case, then it is time to get things separated.

Then I went back to my father's. I told my father that they had sworn to respect, and help me. "If they are the same, when I get back there, then I wouldn't wait just a single day, and I don't care who says what" I told him. He then, told me: "You should do whatever you feel the best. Do not make yourself feel worthless."

One day, my mother wanted me to give her some money to get some needs. I told her "Well, I have almost no money left, and I need to go back. We spent it together, why didn't you tell me before that you need money?" She then said "Wow, look that. Keeping her money away from us?" so she kicked me and my daughter out of the house. I stood there for a while. I needed some time to process what happened. Then I had a plan. I was going to go to the consulate in Ankara, then straight back to Australia. I had had my ticket already, and I would not come back here later. There were buses in the centre, so I told my daughter "Let's go, we need to walk to the bridge." We just started walking, then my brother ran at us. He told me "Do not mind our mother. She is not going to bother you anymore. Let us go back sister". But I told her "I'm going back!" I was night, so he said "I will not let you go anywhere at this time. Please come back!" I was angry, but I went back there. My father was at door.

"If every door is closed on you, this is the only one which open to you every time you need. It is you dad's door; it can't be closed on you. Your father might be poor, but he still can give you whatever he has. So, everything I have, is also yours."

I stood there, and just looked at his eyes. I was sad, and my eyes were in tears. My father had COPD. He was trying his best to get his treatment when he was happy, but sometimes he was rejecting his treatment. He was looking around with eyes that had no desire to live. His condition was changing by his moods.

I spent my last couple days with my father. But it was time to say goodbye, so I went back to Australia. Husband of my husband's sister took me from airport. He told me "Your husband has lots of works to do. But you see him at home". We went to the house; we had our breakfast. They told me there: "We got another house for you; you're not staying here anymore." Is that so? Wow, so much happened apparently... I realised that, there was something wrong again. They took me that house. Furnitures there were all broken, it was a mess. There were dead cockroaches on the kitchen table. We ate roasted chickpeas and raisin for meal. And I had my daughter with me, my beautiful daughter... They were really pushing me, one could easily be a murderer, or a psychopath just because of them... Hopefully, I did not anything wrong, and I am grateful for that. But of course, I told my answers to their faces. I wish that liar father-in-law of mine: "May the god damn him, may the holy Quran damn him." Because he did not even care about religion at all, it was money for him always. It was their plan to hamper my right on court about division of property.

Next day, I went to the social security institution. I found out that they complained about me. They told there; I had had a boyfriend, and I was rich, so that I would not be able to get a help from government. There were only 20 American dollars in my pocket. I managed to spend two days with that money. Some of my neighbours gave testimony, and then some official government workers came at my home, to check the allegations. But thanks to God, they understood my situation, so I, once more, was getting my money. I put myself together in a short period of time. My previous apartment was available. As if my God was helping me... It was a feeling that gave me the courage to continue. It was like a message to me, so I went back to my job.

Apparently, for some; it is also a crime to be an honourable woman. I left there, but I did not receive any notice of appearance from court, so I did not manage to appear at my case that day, and did not assign any attorney. Unfortunately, thanks to this misunderstanding, I was the one facing with foreclosure suit, I was the one who need to pay the money. I was angry. When you left out with no one on your side, who support goodness, act of badness would be three steps ahead.

I was thinking what it was going to happen, while I am on my way to work. I was calling social securities to get some help. I was helping with the tea-coffee service in a tea house. I also got my first car. Things were going great, but the man who tried to take my own money from me, he is the father of my child. One day, on my way to work, I opened the door of my garden. But a different car, came alongside me. A man and a woman got out of the car. That woman came straight to me. And asked me: "So, you're working here?" I told her "Yes?" But I was asking myself who that lady was. She was trying to look straight in my eyes… It was that hard.

I was famous back then in Turkish society. Women back there would see my troubles, and feel angry, so they would try to help me. Other would try to come close to me, to be right in the middle of the action. And some would look at my lonely struggles ecstatically. So, this woman was weird to see. I did not feel comfortable enough to focus on other matters, what I had been gone through was already enough for me. My mental state was at the edge.

I told them they could sit somewhere, because the coffee shop was not open yet. I started my daily work. Woman was coming next to me to talk with me, but I was not listening her. Because I was obsessed with my own problems, I was thinking about what could I do. I was tired both physically and mentally. I was not fond of other people, but I would never swear at them. So, I did not say to her anything. But what was she thinking, what was her reason?

I needed to focus my own work, because I had nothing else at that moment. I was ignoring them, because I was at the edge mentally, and one more incident would be a misery for me. Finally, we started to talked after my work was done. She told me that, she was my mother, and she would have done anything to help me go through these hard moments. She also told me that I was sick, so that I should not have worked at all. But I was not sick at all! I told her that I had not been to a doctor till I came here, and that I was not sick.

"I am so sorry; my intention is not to be mean to you. But please leave me alone. I already have many problems; I need to deal with them. You are wrong, my mother is in Turkey. My family would not lie to me about that important matter."

"No, I am your real mother. They lied to you. Whatever your problems are, we can overcome them together. Look, we all will come to Australia just for you. Please do not be stubborn. You do not have your father, but you have your uncles, you have us."

I was going crazy. I started shaking like crazy. I mean why would my family lie to me about such an important matter? And I was not trying to be stubborn, or anything. I was just trying to do the right thing. Why would I accept a stranger as my mother, why would I take her money? Why would I let others to use me? I would have dealt with my problems, on my own.

"I do not need your help ma'am. My father did not tell me anything about this."

She insisted a lot.

"I am sorry, but you should stop insisting. I asked about this to my father. He told me 'Yes, I had a daughter, but she died,' and my mother told me 'I'm your mother' and my father confirmed that also."

She looked at me:

"So, you love that woman?"

"No, not at all! But I have nothing else to do, she is my mother in the end. I do not know you, and I believe my family would never lie to me. This is the important part. My family would not lie to me!"

My God, I was going crazy! I wanted to go somewhere quiet to scream. My body had shivered for days. There were many people coming back at me, and each one of them were making me tired... I needed to get split, to deal with every matter! I had to work, I needed money. I had to seek for professional help, and I needed to look for a solution. My daughter started the school, so again she also needed to get picked up from school. I was all alone, but everyone was coming back at me, as if they all understood beforehand, like they had no other purposes. What kind of life is that...? And that woman who said my "I'm your real mother", where was she? What happened, so she left me? Of course, I was telling all these to myself, but I did not say a thing to her face. And I would not have done it, even if I had tried. It was so bad that, I was trying to think about everything, I was trying to spell everything, to understand them well. Everyone left me there, did not even think about me, so what... I thought, if I had solved daily matters, I could have tried to deal with bigger ones later. And my mind was always busy about what happened to me. I was reliving what happened before. I was crying at a corner, then trying to consolidate my all by myself. "Don't ever stop fighting, so that you don't make your enemies happy." My best option back then was singing, when I had problems. I heard that back in times, people with mental problems had been treated with music, so maybe that was the case for me. That was my cure, I was even singing, while I was working. I could not care about my own, because of all those problems, and my mental health. Always a problem, always... And what about myself? I was still trying to do the right thing, while I was in the middle of all these madness and wrongs. Why I was focusing on every matter? In the meantime, that woman was still talking to me.

"I would to everything to help you feel in peace. Just listen to me. You are just stubborn, just like your father. You are extremely important for us, look at us. All of us want to come here, just for you, or wherever you want to live."

"I think I am not expressing myself clearly! I do not know you!" I had no idea how to fight against all those problems. I still had many questions on my mind. I was suspicious of my family too. But my father was caring about me. Would a father let his daughter to live a lie? Fortunately, that lady went away, but she was crying. Then my boss came next to me:

"Your mother is crying there; you shouldn't do that to her."

"I don't know her!"

I am still angry at that woman too, because she left me. People always look at problems from their perspectives, but do not care about others... Yes, I would understand, if I had been a kid back then. But am I a puppet? Everyone has their own feelings, characteristics. There should be a procedure to talk those heavy matters. My father was not right, so that I lost two people.

After that talk with that woman, I tried to understand who was lying, and who was right, I thought about it for days. In the meantime, I was doing my best to solve my problems. We went to a lawyer, with my boss' daughter Nergiz. They told me about this, thanks to them. David was an Englishman; he was a great person. I told him about what I was going through. He could not believe it. He told me: "I think I can prove what you told me. And if I managed to do that, we could try something for you. I am going to work on this matter, I will let you know if I find something." And he really did. He saved me from that cruel person. I am still grateful to him. And I cannot forget what he had done for me.

Things were okay now, the only thing that was left was money. I needed to work. So, I started working regularly. First, I dealt with my financial problems. Then I planned to visit my family one again. I bought our tickets, for me and for my daughter, to Türkiye on September of 1996. Again, I tried my best to buy presents for my family, and my relatives. By the way, I was talking with my brothers in İstanbul. So, I went there first. My brother and my sister were in the same building. My father, on the other hand, was in Bafra. My father was sick. COPD really was harsh on him. They told me he had an attack, but hopefully he did not have any attack while I was there.

My brother was business relation, working as a baker. One day a man was at the shop, he asked my brother:

"Who's this lady?" then he told me:

"Welcome."

My brother answered.

"She's, my sister."

"Well, she looks pretty different."

"Yes, she is different. She is both similar, and different than us."

I was just looking at them. I laughed at my brother, because I thought he was making a joke. Then he told me about Azerbaijan and Georgia:

"If you went those countries, you can open a bakery."

"Why? Why would I go to the Azerbaijan?"

"Because you are from there. Not Azerbaijan, but the other one, I mean Georgia. You should ask our father about it when you go back to Bafra. In fact, he wrote a letter about this matter. That is, it from me, my sister." I nodded and told him: "Yes, I'll ask about it." I had some works in İstanbul, after that, I went to Bafra.

My father had missed me so much.

He told me: "Sit next to me during the day, and sleep right next to me at night. So that I can sleep while smelling your beautiful smell. I have missed you so much my beautiful girl. You should see your relatives, but do not spend so much time there, come back immediately. I want to be with you."

Then my mother told me:

"I care about my daughter, and she care about her daughter." But I did not care what she said. Then she said it again. Then I asked her: "Just tell me straight. What do you mean?"

"It is your things. You care about your daughter so much, and I care about you, that is it."

"What is that mean?" I told her. It was like a confession.

"Well... it's like that." She pointed her fingers to my daughter: "It's a shame for her, and for you." So, there was really something weird. It was time to learn about what was going on. I deserved to know it, and make a choice.

I asked my father: "Father, now it is time to tell me the truth. Please do not keep it yourself anymore." He did not say anything, he did not even look at me. He just told "There's nothing to know my girl".

Next day, we went to shopping with my mother. While we were shopping, I saw my childhood friend he was just had his own business. I told him: "Congratulations, hopefully you earn well." He answered me: "Thank you." Then he told me: "My sister is also in İstanbul. And you go there also. Let me give you her phone number. So that you can talk. She will be happy to see you." And I said "Okay." He gave her sister's phone number, as well as the numbers of other childhood friends of ours. Then I went to İstanbul again. And called each one of them. We had so much fun talking. It was good for me to speak with all these people, even though we did not see each other in real life.

There was a problem about one of my properties. I called the police, and stated a complaint about it. Hopefully, thanks to the District Governorship of Bahçelievler İstanbul, I managed the solve the problem easily. So, another problem was also solved. Then I went to Bafra again. But I learned that there was a gossip about me. Apparently, I called our neighbour's son, to seduce him. But I called the police, I did not know it was him. I told about it to my father. He understood me well, and believed me. But my mother said:

"You believe your daughter, but I saw it with my eyes, she took his number from Remzi."

I was shocked to hear that. She was telling lies, right in front of my face. I told her: "You always say that you have a hearing problem. But shockingly, you talk about what you even did not hear. How do you do that, I ask you! I only got my girlfriends' numbers from Remzi. And even Remzi is the witness of it. You can ask him. You are keep telling me that you are my mother. But a mother cannot tell such lies about her daughter, or even about a stranger. You should be ashamed."

I was angry, ashamed, and uncomfortable. Because everybody would always believe her just because she was my mother. I could not control myself anymore, in these kinds of incidents. That woman cannot be a mother! My father understood what was going on, and was sad about it.

My father had bought some lands with his money. But he asked my help about his debts. Of course, I accepted it, because my father had no one else to ask for help. His sickness was making me sad. Then my mother said: "So, you accepted it. There might be problems, but we are a family in the end. You are important to us." But she was trying to be nice at me, just because I decided to help them. But my behaviours had already changed towards her. I was sure that she was telling lies intentionally.

I told my father: "Yes, I am your daughter, and it is my duty as a daughter to help you. But if you have anything to tell me, please tell me. You told me that this woman is my real mother, but she cannot be. She cannot be my mother." He did not say anything.

Later that night my aunt's husband, and son of my father's uncle came to visit us. They visited us to see both me and my father. That night, I slept on the sofa, right next to my father's. I was sleeping still, but I woke up. I was completely under the blanket. So, it was impossible for them to see me. My aunt was awake, probably for her morning prayer. My father was also awake. After the prayer, they started talking.

My father told my aunt: "She's getting suspicious, I'm really sad." And then she told him: "What do you think to do? Will you let her go to her mother? But of course, like they say 'Even an animal can feel her own mother.' But her mother... She is just an infidel."

I went straight up. I told them "What are you talking about?" They just told me "Nothing, we were just talking."

It was time for breakfast. Then that day passed away just like that. That night, I slept in the same sofa. My father was also doing his morning prayers. I looked at him. Then I realised someone was sitting in another sofa. I was my grandpa. He looked at me and smiled at me. But then he looked at my father in a very angry way. I jumped out of my bed. My father asked "What happened?"

"Oh father... I felt him completely... My grandpa was here, he was smiling at me, but he looked at you angrily. Then he just faded away."

My father prayed a bit, then he just looked at me in a sad way.

"Father, why my grandpa is still angry at you? What is going on? Can you please tell me?"

My father did not say anything, just like before. Then we had our breakfast. My mother was doing the chores in other room.

Then my father told me "Okay, I have my decision. I will tell you everything. Come here." I went to him. It was the day of truth for my dad.

"I was called and warned. I will not see you again, as a live human being, and I do not think I have much time left. I am not sure, but probably when you come here on more time in the future, you will see my death body, or my grave. And, yes. There is something I need to tell you. I will tell you the truth, but I want no questions. I will tell you only whatever I want... Because I made a promise, you are my daughter, till I die. So, in order to be my daughter till the end of my life, I will only tell you the truth." He wanted me to swear, so I swore.

"I trust your word. I do not know you noticed it before, but I live this life with you. You are the reason of my life, your visit to me. But I know, my days are counting now. I saw it in a dream. So, now it is my time to tell you the truth. But you will listen only." Then he started. It was not an easy thing to do for a father. His face was red overall.

"As you might remember, we went to Samsun, to a court, and gave our statements... That woman who complained about us, is your real mother. Woman from Australia... She did really want to have you, and did nothing wrong. You were sick. So, we decided to take you here to father place. I went to Germany, to work. We met there, with your mother. We became friends almost immediately. Then our friendship had grown, and we wanted to get married. Your mother was Russian, & Greek, and I am a Turk, and Muslim. So, they did not want us to get married. But then your mother insisted so much. They accepted it in one condition. They wanted us to get married in a church.

I thought about it a bit, but we had no options, so I accepted it. They changed my name; they named me Mikail. Because it was both a Christian and Muslim name. And I and your mother got married in a church. Your mother took refuge in Germany. So, she used Margared as her name back there, but I was calling her Meryem."

Weird thing was that I wanted him to tell me the truth, but I was not comfortable with it. I felt like there were hammers on my mind. I was having quakes on my mind. I heard what my father told me, but those words were flying away. The story was not the one to enjoy, it made me sad.

"I do not know if your mother would ever come back. But if she comes, be nice to her. She is your mother. I know, I should have told you that way before, but just like I told you, I was going to lose you, if ever told you that. You would not have come back at me, and I would have been devastated."

He continued.

"We were living in a small town, in Munich. Your mother was pregnant to you back then, and she would go to examinations regularly. There was a friend of hers who worked in the clinic that your mom would go. You were born in Bogen Hausens, Munich. Nurses did not leave you at all, you were at their hands, because you were extremely cute, and beautiful. Your mother was working, so she only managed get a 2-weeks off from her job. After two weeks, she started working again, and I took care of you for a whole month. But you were sick. We would take you to hospital almost every day. Doctor told us that you had an allergy for cold weathers. So, he suggested us to take you somewhere warm, and raised you there until you age were two or three. It was September. Doctor told us "It is only September, but she is already not in good condition. She cannot make it in winter." So, we were devastated to hear that. We were shocked, and did not know what to do. Then we thought about it. We could not have taken you to your grandmother's. Because where she lived was also very cold. The only solution was to take you to my mother's. Your mother was sad to hear that, she cried a lot. But accepted it because she wanted you to live. It was time to start my job again, so I thought I would have taken you to my mother, and went back to Germany. I spoke with one of my friends, who had a car. So, we took his car, and I took you to Turkey. It was Thursday, and we were in Bafra in noon of Friday. My beloved mother was really surprised to see me, but she was happy in the end. I told you about my mother, they were already familiar with the case. So, they took you. I had not changed your diaper, because we were almost there. You were dirty. But I did not care it, I kissed you, and handed you to my mother. There were no one at house, women were at field, and men were at mosque. My mother cooked for us. While I was eating, she bathed you. You were as clean as heaven. When I decided to go back, you were sleeping. But as if you felt it, you started crying immediately. I felt terrible. But we had no other chance my girl. That was the case. You must promise me, after my death, you need to find your mother. I told you what happened, but you will get the relevant information about your mother after my death. So, please find you mother then."

I was not sure what just happened, where was I, what was I doing, I was really in a bad condition. My mind was not on me... Where was I? Where was my mind? Where was my body? When

I was on street, I was walking to the places, that I have never seen before. I was always thinking about it. I was sad about my mother. It was hard to choose between a father and a mother. I loved my father, even though he was wrong, because he was my father. When he made a mistake, he would do that by ignorance, it was unintentional. So, just like everyone else, he made lots of mistakes. My father was always angry, and aggressive. But in that moment, I realised that all the things he went through made him what he was as a person. Those problems made him sad, pushed him to other problems, and so he could not cope with them.

I still did not manage to solve the puzzle that I was inside. There were still many questions. That is why, I had to find my mother, because she was my real mother. But I swore about it, and gave my word to my father. But how did all these happen? Should I have wanted my father's death, just to find my real mother? How could I such a thing? I loved my father... It was again a course of time like hell...

After that talk, I went to Australia three weeks later. I had to work, to pay my dad's debts. I was praying to see my mother one more time, but she never came back. Wish she would have come back again, so that I would have had the opportunity to tell her everything. These thoughts were on my mind all the time. Still, it was a secret, but still it was eating me alive. After that much, finally I managed to get some answers, but I was still away from my mother.

I went back to Australia, and started looking for job opportunities. I needed to pay my debt immediately. So, I started working again. Daily tasks, and my own problems were making my mind busy. I was a nervous wreck, my mental health was not in the ideal condition, and my mind was tired to think all the time. But no matter what happened to me, working was my priority. Because, thanks to my jobs, I could deal with it, and made myself busy with it, so that I could forget about all my problems. That secret my dad shared with me, was too heavy to carry. I had lost my mother.

Many agonizing days was spent there, and I waited for justice. I had many enemies that I did not even know them, or their causes. I was aware of them, but I was not aware the damage they could have done on me. I saw them just the result of simple jealousy. It must have been someone strong in our family to have that letter my dad wrote to me! My dad gave it to him, so he must have trusted him. Oh, my God! I was not even controlling myself anymore. I needed happiness back then, so I was telling myself jokes so just have a proper laugh. But in the end, many problems and absence in my life would fill my eyes with tears. People around me were aware of my sadness, but they were thinking I was sad just because we were divorced with my husband. But they did not aware of the hurricanes inside me, but I also had a peaceful side too.

I did not talk about this matter to anyone, just because I swore about it. I made a promise. But still I wanted to know more things, one part of mine were about my daughter, but the other one was all about my mother, I had looked after her always. And I was always alert about that matter, just to find out more details about my mother. There were many people that I was mistaken about, and I was in doubt. Just because I thought she was my mother... Tensions, and agitations... My God, help me!

My father's debts were finally over, but they kept asking money from me. My father told me: "You do not like me anymore. But you should send me your money. You earn well, so let us have that money to save it. We can open a shop here." It was probably that woman who provoked my father, but I was angry at them. I lost my control because of their weird actions, weird, and selfish actions. But I did not say anything bad to my father, just because I did not want him to think that way.

"I trust you so much. And I paid your debt, for a dead investment that I will probably never use in the future. And to do that, I spent 3 hours in the road, just because I wanted to paid all your debts, so that you would not feel bad about it. But you are trying to put even more responsibilities on me. I do not deserve that! How do you want something like that? I am just a woman, but all of you, my mother, and my father are just looking at my hand for their own future. How do you want such a thing? How do you expect from me to be the 'warrantor' of everybody's life? You do not even care how I earn that money; it does not matter for you. You cannot treat me like a dog, for your own life. Take it, or leave it, it is up to you. That is, it from me! I neither pay your debt, nor send you any money anymore. You made me marry with that man when I was just a little girl. You hindered all my dreams about studying. And you are asking for money now, how happy I should be right?!"

My father was regretful after my answer.

"I'm so sorry my beautiful girl, I just made a mistake." But I did not stop there.

"You are telling me about my real mother. But you are keeping me away from the information of where she is. I am not in good condition both mentally and physically, just because I am your daughter. Do you even care about me a little, what I am dealing with here dad?"

In Sydney, near Central Station, there was a Greek coffee shop and sandwich house. I worked at there for a time. They all were great people, they helped me so much, and taught me about the details of job. I worked there for a long time.

One day my daughter told me: "Mom, I feel it, my grandpa is sad. You should call him, he even apologized from you." And I told her: "Yes, you are right, I just waited to get calm a bit. I will call him." And so, I called my father. I was our last talk with my father. "My daughter, you called me, thank you for that. We were angry at each other, but now we are good. I am happy to see this day, even though I will day soon." But I was sad to hear that: "Dad, do not say that. I do not want you to die. I want you to be happy, and fine. I want you to live." We both apologized each other. I was at peace after that talk.

Later, I got an offer for partnership. I was not so open about it. I told them "I can't work as partners, there would always be problems in it." But they insisted so much, and did not even leave my house until I accepted it. They were from Samsun. We were both friends, and neighbours. Finally, I said "I'm convinced," and left my job. I had to pay some money to start a partnership. I had to withdraw some cash from bank that day. I was getting ready when I heard my daughter's scream. She was trying to pick up a towel from our balcony.

"Oh, mom! It is scary!"

"What? What is scary?"

"Just come here!"

There was a huge owl on the laundry line. It did not even get scared when it saw us. It was looking right in my eyes. Hope the best... We took another towel that day. When we left our house, that owl was still on that line.

I withdrew the needed money. I was going to the attorney, but I had heard about bad news. My father was in coma, and they were asking me. It was a nightmare for me. The thought about my father's death was scary. I was about to lose my consciousness. They took the money I was holding.

It was the year 2000, and 10th of January. My uncle's son Veli was keeping me notified. "Maybe he will get better. Why do you always think about death?" He was saying things like that, but next, he told me:

"Sister, I could not tell you but my uncle has passed away... Let us buy your ticket immediately, so you can go there." I was crying, I left the shopping mall. I met with Veli, and we bought my ticket. My flight was in two hours, so I needed to be urgent to catch it. I was getting ready and saying goodbye to other while I was crying. It was a 24 hours flight, and each minute I was thinking about memories of my father. I cried every bit second of that flight. I was crying under a blanket not to make others uncomfortable, but people around me was asking: "What happened? Do you need help?" I told them: "Unfortunately, you cannot do anything about it. My father's dead. I am going to his funeral. I do not want to make you feel uncomfortable here, but I am about cry." One of the passengers told me: "I am not uncomfortable at all. I am so sorry to hear that." I just thanked him.

We talked about my aunt's son Erdem. He was going to get me from airport, when I landed in İstanbul. When I got there, the airport has entered service just couple of days before. It was nine at night. I could not find a single telephone to call Erdem. I asked couple of shops, but no one helped me about it. But then I saw a security guard team, so I told them what happened. "I am here for the funeral of my dad. I left my house in a hurry. I need to get in touch with my relatives, so could you please help me?" Commander of that them gave me a telephone coin, and showed me the telephone box. I wanted to pay for the coin, but he told me "It's not necessary, I'm sorry to hear about your lost."

It was winter, and I only had a jacket on me. My eyes were all red because of tears. I was all messy. Anyway, I managed to make that call. So, we were on the road again. We went to Çarşamba with plane. On the exit of the airport, a woman in Customs Control told me "You cannot exit the airport without an identity card. Otherwise, you need to pay 110 TL". It was midnight... "Okay, but do you have an ATM, or EFTPOS so that I can pay with my credit card?" but she said; "No, we don't have. And you do not have your id on you as well."

"What about my passport? Isn't that some kind of identity? I travelled many countries, I was just in İstanbul, and had no problem anywhere. So, why do you make a scene suddenly? I am here for my dad's funeral, and I do not have a cash on me. I can pay with dollars. You can take my credentials or address, and we can deal with it later, if that is okay for you. Please... My relatives are waiting for me, I am here for a funeral!"

But that woman was insisting about paying in cash and in Turkish liras. But I was full of it. "What kind of nonsense is that? Are there no police here? I am not a murderer, or a fugitive! I want to complain about this maniac who wants the impossible from in the middle of the night! Please, can someone come here to help me? No one?"

But then police came towards us to intervene. "I'm here to help ma'am." Then he said that woman: "Don't you have any respect for a dead? Don't you see she is crying? She has a funeral to attend!" Then he took the receipt from that woman and ripped it off, and said that woman again: "If anyone tomorrow want this money, then you'll pay it!"

May God bless his soul… Finally, after an hour, I managed to get out of customs office at 1 am. I said that police: "I do not know you, but you are a great person. May God help you!" he replied: "You should go now, sorry for your lost."

After I went out of airport, one of my cousins came next to me: "Sister, where have you been? We are waiting for hours." We greeted each other, and hopped in the car. It was a two-hour road ahead to go there. I told about what happened to them in the car. And they told me that they buried my father, but there were many people who are waiting for me at house. It was three in the morning. Finally, after 33 hours of travel, I was at home. My mother, brother, and my cousins were still awake. They were waiting for me. My mother started crying when she saw me. "You came for your father" she said. I hugged everyone; we were all very sorry. We talked a bit. Then my uncle said: "Even though it is almost morning, you should get some sleep. People start coming here in the morning to express their condolences, so you should be okay to greet them."

All of us went our beds, but I could not sleep. I was still shaken on my dad's death. My father was not in our house now, neither as alive, nor as death. It was the morning prayer time, so everyone was up. Condolences, condolences... My grandpa and my grandma were also there, I mean my mother's step mom and step dad. They told me: "Come on, up now. You should perform an ablution, so that we can go to the graveyard. We buried your father in afternoon prayer. We should pay him a visit." I just said "Okay grandpa". So, we went to the graveyard.

I had 'Yasin' book with me, it was a book consists of thirty-six sure of the Quran. I read that book to my father. It was freezing out there and weather was snowy. My hand was almost going to freeze, but I did not stop. They were just there to take me to the grave. My mother and her step mother... She was not my mother too; she was also my step mother. She made fun of me, because I was reading that book in Turkish. In other words, it had no meaning for her, because it was in Turkish... But my grandpa told me "Do not care about her my girl. You should read it however you want. In the end, it is for your mother".

I prayed for my dad, I cried, I saw his grave, now it was time to go back. When we got back to our house, our guests were coming also. We all prayed that day. A hodja from mosque was here almost every day in the following days to pray and read Quran. We did not sleep again that night, and we had long talks. Things got quite a bit, so I fell asleep. It was my first proper sleep in three days.

My father picked me up to put me in my bed, and I got awake that moment. But I did not even want to get up. People were praying for my dad, but I could not get up, so I did not pray that night.

It was next morning, and I woke up. But I still was not myself. People were still visiting us. It was a tradition; people would come to the funeral home for months. It was my third day at that house, and again there were many guests. Later that night, our relatives decided to stay with us. We all were sleeping on sofas. My grand-aunt was also with us, and I was sleeping next to the heating stove, because I was sensitive to cold weather... Before we all fall asleep, I started thinking about my father. As if I was speaking with him.

Why did you leave me dad? What are you doing now, where are you? Rest in peace. Wish you were here, and tell me about my mother...

Just at that moment, a light beam started to come into view. I looked through it. It was in the shape of a human. That light told me:

"Do not be scared! Stay calm. I am the angel who is your right hand. They did not wait long enough to show your father to you. But I have someone here, that you want to see." He held my chin, and showed me the left side of the room. There was something like a curtain, from that moment I was not able to see what was going on in that room. On the left-hand side, there was a man and a girl who is very similar to me... My father was waiting on a washtub to perform an ablution, and that girl was pouring the water. After that, he started walking towards me. He was like a cloud in distant, but as he kept walking towards me, he was in the shape of himself. He looked like my father. He told me:

"My dearest girl, I was not expecting you, but here you are. I saw that you were here. Do not you worry about me, I am all fine. I am still around here. You were in my grave, you prayed for me. Those prayers made things fine for me, my beautiful daughter. You should always pray for me."

I was sitting there all speechless. I was calm, but was still shocked. We were not talking vocally; it was like a communication via our minds. My father continued:

"You read 'Yasin' prayer for me, but it was cold, so you could not pray the sura of 'Ameneresulü'. Now, let us pray together, shall we?"

"But father, I have to perform an ablution to pray."

"I just made that for you. It is all okay, do not you worry."

"But I don't know that sura dad." Then I looked at the angel on our right side.

It told me: "Don't you worry, you'll be able to pray with us." And so, I prayed with my dad. My dad made some mistakes about me, but he was also the victim of different problems. They asked me: "Do you give your blessing to your father?" I looked at them, and asked them: "Who are you? Where am I?" They told me:

"You are not with us yet, but you will be here. We are here as messengers of the invisible world. We have things to tell you: You are in danger. They upset you. You fear death, but death is not something to fear. The real danger, is in the world you live now. When you come to us in future, we will keep you safe from every danger. No one can even touch you, if we do not allow it. And if you are willing to come here, we can take you now." Then my father started begging.

"Come here my girl. And we can take your mother, so that we can live in peace."

But I told him: "No, I have a daughter who needs me, I can't leave her alone."

Angels told me: "Then we allow you to stay in that world, you already have some time to live there. But they are trying to fool you. They will not tell you the address of your mother. And maybe you will be unable to find your mother. But when it is your time to come here, your mother will be the first person you will meet."

"Why don't you help me to find my mom, when I'm already alive?"

"We allow you to do whatever you want about that. But it is up to you. It is between God and you."

"Please, help me to find my mom, I beg you!"

"We will submit your request."

In the meantime, my aunt started calling my name. I raised my hand to stop her, because I did not want to end that conversation. The angel right in front of me said:

"Do not care about them. They are all sinners. Their actions were the ones who were forbidden for this holy religion. You tell them, they all will see the consequences of their badness. This family will be devastated in the future. But it is our time to go."

"What about me? Will I be ever managed to find my mom?"

"Maybe."

"But how?"

"Maybe with technology."

Then my brother came towards me. He shook me to awake me. But I was in peace in that moment. I was alone, but I had the feeling that my father was with me there.

"What happened to you? What were you saying?"

"I did not do anything. My father came, and talked with me." Then my step-mother started to cry and scream, because she was scared. I just looked at her eyes, then I remembered all the stuff she did to me; all that badness, all those bad memories from my childhood. I remembered my childhood...

Next day, first thing, I asked about my father's belongings. I was going to look for that letter. My sister, and I went to Bafra, to my father's place. She showed me the belongings of my father, then handed me a photo. She told me furiously: "Here, take it. That was inside his pocket. There is no letter, or anything. Why are you making things up?" But I told her what my father told me.

"His mind was perplexed in his sickness. But there is no letter, or anything, do not make things up." I did not have an argument with her, because we were mourning. But unfortunately, I did not have enough time. I signed couple of documents for official procedures, and went back to Australia.

When I went back, I found out that my partner had sold his shares to someone else. So, I had a new partner. I had to make business with people who did not have the common sense and lie all the time. That new partner did not want to start the business immediately, so we could not start the official procedures. But then we went to court, and we decided to undertake the procedures. During that time, my aunt Aysel come here from Türkiye. Her son was in Australia, so she was here to have a nice vacation. I asked her about my mother. She told me:

"You should close that case now. It would only make you even sadder. Do not be sad about everything, you should stop doing it."

"You know where she is, but still trying to cover it. That is what makes me sad." I told her about what my father told me before his death:

"I am still waiting after my dad's death. Who has that letter, and who will explain to me what is going on? What you are doing now is a huge mistake... I still see my dad in my dreams, since the day of his funeral. He kept telling me to find my mother. It also makes my dad uncomfortable; he needs peace where he is now. You should keep your promise."

"Who is my mother? Why do you keep it away from me?"

"I do not know. We had many problems back in time, it was a shame for us. So, you should leave it there."

I could not insist more. Yes, she really had many problems in her marriage. But how can I forget about my mother? It is not something to forget.

"Maybe you know something. But whoever has the knowledge about her, just tell me his name. I am onto this cause; I am not going to leave it. I will find my mother. I want to resolve this problem inside our family. I do not want anyone to get hurt. I do not know almost anything about this problem. So, it can be solved inside our family with another problem. Just give me some information about my mother." She just said "Okay".

It was time to go for my aunt. So, she went back to Türkiye. But I did not receive any news about it. After that, I called her.

"Who is my mother? I know I have a mother. My father is now dead, but he keeps telling me to find her in my dreams. And you all will also die one day just like my father. Don't you want to get rid of that sin? What is wrong?"

She answered me:

"Oh, my dear. I did not see your mother at all. She never came here. Your father took you here, you were just a little baby. It was less then forty days of your birth; you were that small. I do not want to die with this sin, but that was a secret. Why your father told you about it? Maybe your uncle knows about your mother. Let us ask him." Her husband uncle Yusuf were cousins with my father. She told me when he would have been at home, so I called them again.

But uncle Yusuf told me: "There are no such a thing. Your mother is Makbule. She raised you; she is your mother. I cannot say anything about this without her permission. That is, it."

"It's not over for me uncle, it is not."

The year was 2005. I went to Türkiye to talk about this with my brother. He told me: "So, you're saying you're just the bastard of my father?"

"If the children whose mother are known are the bastards, then you're also a bastard!"

"No, I was just messing with you. Let me ask my mother, but I have only one condition, I will also come with you to see your mother."

I was surprised to hear that. I had not seen my mother before. I had not known what she was like. I was nervous about everything. I had to find my mother; I was her daughter. She would not have hurt me. But why did my brother want to come with me, to visit my own mother? I was not fond of his idea. Anyway, he talked with his mother. His mother told him: "I am sad to hear that. There is no such a thing. Her father was almost mad, so she still believes him." God help me... I was aware that there was a collective lie against me. But why all of them were so strict about it? I mean, what was the problem about me finding my real mom?

My brother, and my sister were following me again. Where I am going, what I am doing... They were trying to control me. And they were also dealing with spells. They were doing plans like a jinni. I was feeling like a fool, as if my head was heavier than my body. My mind was slow, it was so slow that, I was having problems to remember people. I was almost their captive. My mom was telling other that I was in this condition because I was left without a husband. Yes, my mind was slow, but I did not lose it yet. I was aware of their traps and lies against me.

One day I was sick and was sleeping on my bed. She came towards me and told me:

"Breakfast is ready, get up!" So, I got up, and went to the kitchen. There were only olives on table. That was the breakfast she told me. I just looked at her face and asked: "So, breakfast?" She laughed and said: "Well open that fridge. There is some leek in it. You wash them, and cook them in butter, with black pepper and salt. And do not forget to make me tea, then the breakfast is ready!" I took the leek from fridge. I washed it, and chopped it. She was watching me in joy. I put it in the pan, and some salt on it. But I also put a pepper right in front of her. I told her "You are going to eat it now. Then I will take you to the bathroom, and I will wash you with cold water, just like you washed me before. Come on eat it." She took it, and then I went to bathroom. But she called her child to get my brother.

When I was out of the bathroom there were no one in house. Just a little later, my brother came with my sister.

"Hmm, it was effective for 40 days. We should do it again.

"What's that?" I asked him.

"The talisman."

"For whom?"

"For you."

"So, you're messing with me, and saying that right into my face?"

"Sister, you have always loved our mother, but you are obsessed with her now. There is something wrong."

God help me... As if his mother was something to love.

The year was 2006. I was once again in İstanbul to find some answers. They called me, and said "I and your uncle's wife Mahmure found someone who was a friend with your father in Germany, we will take you her." I told him "Well, thanks brother." And again, one day, I was in a bus, going somewhere. Someone called me. It was my aunt. I answered it, but no one was speaking with me. I waited a bit to understand. There were two women talking.

Mahmure was talking about her trap to my aunt:

"We are not going to tell her who her mother is. She should just seek for her like a madman. To convince her I found two friends of her father from Germany. One of them did not agree with me, but other agreed. So, I am going to make her speak with him."

My aunt told her: "Why don't you just tell her the truth? If you take her to me, I will tell her the truth, I can't tell anymore lies."

"Her mother just got divorced with his second husband. She left Germany, and went to her father's hometown. So, she can see her mother in her dreams!"

"But she already knows the truth, why do you keep telling lies?"

"That's what Mete Aga wants from us."

There was almost no lie left that I did not hear from them. I went to Samsun in the end of Ramadan fest. I was not speaking with my uncle. But my brother took me to his house, without telling me anything. There, they tried to make me eat some dolma. But inside it there was something. They forced me to eat it. I ate it first, but thrown up later. It got stuck in my gullet. It was the special gift of Mahmure... Then I got sick.

They took me some man named Adem. They told me lies, right straight to my face. But I told them what my father told me.

"That was a secret. A secret that I cannot never know. But I will. I cannot tell you are lying, but what I told you is all truth." We left Adem's office. I was with my both uncles, and Mahmure. I have never felt anger to a human being than I felt about her. She was the most unreliable and liar person I had even seen in my life. Lies I heard from them was shaken me for sure, but I was still on the road of truth, and I had no desire to just give up.

One day I met with my aunt Aysel by chance. She told me: "You should forget about it my girl." But I told her: "You should do at least one favour to me. I do not want anything else. You should stop lying. I heard what you and Mahmure talked over the phone. You kept talking about me on my back, but lying on my face. Don't you ever love me? What did I do to deserve this behaviour?"

My aunt said: "But I told them the tell her the truth, and they did not listen me. My God, I did not even touch that phone, that day. It was on the table. My dear God..."

"Yes, my dear God... It is his justice, even though you all lie to me. But you are still lying to my face, even though our God wants the opposite. A person who does not care about our God's acts can't be a religious person, and can't be my relative."

We could not figure this matter out in our family. So, right now this case is on court. I was trying to find the truth legally. I cannot forget those who I called family that tried to even poison me, and tried to harm me both mentally and materially.

One can lose himself in the middle of that group of people, that is not just. I just want to look ahead now. When I just look at back, I realised that I did really a good and a hard job to stand against all the hardship of this life that I lived.

Yes, some does not lie, but they can protect the liar. Maybe that means they are not liar, but that does not mean they do not help them. Whoever helps the badness and liars, and does not care about the truth and the decent people, cannot be respected. Adults should be just, and act fairly, that should be one of their main traits. Keeping yourself true, and always telling the truth just brings you the peace you need. But if one keeps the truth to himself, and does not do anything about liars, he can cause huge disrupts in social, and family life, he cannot be trusted anymore, and he just crushed everything around him.

No one is alone in this life. And no one is left out of options. No child should be the main subject of the fights of adults. No child can be accused about problems of his childhood. Real offenders are the ones who needed to raise him in a good way. If parents managed to give their children proper senses, then they can protect their children from bad intentions also.

Kids are the gifts that we have received from God. And it does not matter if he is your kid, or others. If we can raise them in a decent way, and teach them the value of justice, then we can live in peace in future.

Laws and media

I was faced with the terrible character of my stepmother and siblings asking for more money for my mother's information. after this outrageous behaviour I faced. I applied to the court. I searched 3 times through a lawyer for the court information that my mother complained about my father, unfortunately the documents were cleared. At first, I could not understand this painful side of the job, so what can be so much effort to keep a mother and her daughter apart, what is the reason for being so cruel?

It turns out that there are other powers that want a mother and a daughter to be separated that have the power to clear court papers. My concerns about my biological mother have increased. Who and how can prevent my mother from visiting me again?

At the same time, I had to spend some time with my brothers and stepmother during my Türkiye holiday in order to be able to talk to them. maybe there is a solution. I was telling me that they were calling me that they did not know about the letter my father left me, at the same time I was being told that they were harming my health and I was facing the most painful facts of my life. I saw that they were enemies to me enough to want me dead.

After getting tired of these psychological pressures, I filed a maternity case. I asked for DNA maternity test and kinship denial at legal medical centre. The court decision gave me 2 months and asked me to present my mother, whom I was looking for for DNA test, to the court as evidence.

(I draw your attention!) the court judge asking my mother, whom I am looking for, to the court as evidence. it's like he's making fun of me.

Despite all these injustices I have experienced, I did not give up. My legal search and lawsuits continue. The missing search TV programs that I reached were helpful and arrogant rather than making my voice heard, the same answer was given, the question is, can you give your mother's identity information?

Sorry, I would like to give you my mother's identity information, but it was not given to me because my father took me away from my mother when I was a baby and I saw pressure that my mother's identity information was never shared with me. My mother's relatives are in Türkiye, so if I make my voice heard on your program, I can reach my mother or those who know her. The answer is unfortunately we cannot help you without your credentials. This answer I got from few TV shows in Türkiye really pissed me off because the answer was to make fools of people and disrespect. Turkish ID's have all the direction information of the city and neighbourhood where people live. It is as easy as pressing two buttons to reach the person whose identity information you know.

Being disrespectful to such an important situation of people, not being realistic, was extremely sickening in the name of humanity.

On the other hand, I reached the German consulate because my father and mother lived in Germany and I was born there. At first, the woman who answered the phone on my first call, said that it is wrong to call us about your subject, we are not interested in these issues, and it almost turnoff the phone to my face! I said do not do that I will keep calling. listened to me and then gave some information. At the same time, I received an email from the German consulate in Ankara. Your problem is that we cannot share your family information with you due to human rights reasons. For all information about the Turkish state, you should contact the Turkish government institutions, they can help you.

I sent an email to the German Turkish consulate, the Berlin embassy, but at first, I could not get a response. There was no response from the berlin embassy. When I wrote to the Munich Turkish consulate again, the answer came, I was just getting my feet, but suddenly, the correspondence stopped. I could not make news in any important Turkish newspaper; I was not allowed.

When I wrote to the Munich Turkish consulate again, I got a reply, just as I was getting it, the correspondence stopped. and at the same time, I could not make news in any important Turkish newspaper, I was not allowed. Sir, I got the answer from the newspaper that it is not a subject worth reporting on. The fact that I was looking for my mother was not considered important by some people and institutions.

wow, the orphans are so lonely and unprotected even by the law.

what a sad truth....

Then there was a revival in my memory, I remembered some subjects. When my father took me to Turkey for the first time, my father had another daughter, this information is available in the family records, but he was personally hidden from the society, my father confessed this to me, but I could not believe it until I saw it with my own eyes. My memory was upset, probably due to the damage done, and as a result of the traumas I went through.

After my father delivered me to my grandmother and left the house, my father mother put me and my older sister on the bed side by side and while we were both sleeping, one of the household members went to the two sleeping babies and changed our blankets. Our faces are covered so that flies do not come in. And my stepmother comes from the field and gets angry when she learns that my father had a second marriage and had a daughter from this marriage. When things calm down, she goes to the babies and wants to kill she is stepdaughter and sits on it.and another baby starts screaming and starts to cry.

Again, one of the family members senses the strange situation and runs to save the baby. When they pushed her away and took the baby, Husniye was a baby, so she accidentally killed her own baby.

and they buried the baby in secret. and they put me in the place of Husniye baby against everyone.

And finally, considering all the information I have given by writing all this information to the necessary institutions, I still want to wait for the necessary sensitivity and importance to reach my real mother.

I am over 50, and have a calm life now. 9 years ago, even though it was a bit late, I managed to have a proper job. I finished the course of cosmetologist. My daughter, on the other hand, is a successful woman, who is studying her third master degree. Our lives just flow away, even though we face with hardship. We have no other goal than to leave a proper and a decent life, and it is a need for our own health.

And I am still looking for my mother. I am trying to fix something that was ruined before. I do not care who was she when she gave birth to me; whether she was married, or not. I am looking for her, just because she is, my mother. I am not in a place to judge her personality. I am responsible about her, just because I am her daughter. Naturally, every child has a mother and a father. A woman, or a father should be ashamed, if he/she ever leave his/her own children, and go away, but not the child.

After my father past, I have been struggling for 23 years to reach my mother. I would like to say that it is very disturbing for humanity that everywhere they block my way to my mother. and at the same time, I would like to point out that it is very clear and very disturbing that the evidence was lost even though there was a court held in Türkiye, although my father went through not one but several customs checks while he was taking me from Germany to Türkiye.

Everyone has a different story to tell about their life, and we all get different experience what we have seen. In order to protect our love against each other, we should always be respectful. Respect is the resource of love. And love is the cure of human soul...

My best regards...

-Hamiye Oksuz.

www.ingramcontent.com/pod-product-compliance
Lightning Source LLC
Chambersburg PA
CBHW050317010526
44107CB00055B/2280